NORTH ATLANTIC
SHOREBIRDS

ear-coverts

crown

nape

eye-ring

hindneck

forehead

side of neck

lore

mantle

nostril

scapulars

lesser coverts

median coverts

bill (upper and
lower mandibles)

greater coverts

tertials

primaries

chin and throat

foreneck

tail

breast

flank

undertail-coverts

tibia

belly

vent

knee

inner

tarsus

middle

toe

hind toe

outer

Frontispiece: Purple
Sandpiper *first-
winter*, to show
plumage and bare-
part terminology.
E England, early
April. *RJC* See also
Fig. 1, p. 24.

THE FACTS ON FILE FIELD GUIDE TO

NORTH ATLANTIC SHOREBIRDS

Richard J. Chandler

A Photographic Guide
to the Waders of Western Europe
and Eastern North America

Facts On File

New York • Oxford

Facts On File, Inc.
460 Park Avenue South
New York, New York 10016

Library of Congress Catalog Card Number 88-046179

British Library Cataloguing in Publication Data

Chandler, R.J.
   North Atlantic shorebirds
   1.   Northern hemisphere. Shorebirds
   I.   Title
   598'.33

   ISBN 0-333-45880-X

Facts On File books are available at special discounts when purchased in
bulk quantities for businesses, associations, institutions, or sales promotion.
Please contact the Special Sales Department at 212/683-2244.
(Dial 1-800-322-8755, except in NY, AK, HI)

Printed in Spain

10 9 8 7 6 5 4 3 2 1

This book is printed on acid-free paper.

CONTENTS

INTRODUCTION

If you have ever listened to the evocative song of a curlew on an upland moor, watched the precision of the co-ordinated aerial manoeuvres of a flock of knots above a winter estuary, or marvelled at the globe-spanning migration of a Sanderling, you will have succumbed, however briefly, to the attraction of shorebirds. This book is dedicated to all those who have fallen under that spell.

Shorebirds – or 'waders' – may be defined as the bird species in the suborder Charadrii. They are small to medium-sized birds that often feed at or near the water's edge or by wading in the shallows. While estuaries and other coastal environments are the most typical of their various habitats, particularly outside the breeding season, shorebirds can also be found in arctic tundra, temperate moorland, damp woodland, the steppes and prairies, tropical savanna, and even in near-desert. Thus, on a global basis, they are a widespread and successful group which, though usually living in open habitats, can on occasion be found far from water.

Although a good deal is now known about shorebirds, including their identification, breeding, feeding ecology, migration, plumages and moult sequences, a great deal remains to be discovered; and therein lies another of the attractions of the group. In one subject area, that of identification and moult studies, many advances have been made in the last ten to fifteen years. This book aims to bring together, for both the general birder and the shorebird enthusiast, these advances as they apply to the shorebirds that occur around the N Atlantic, illustrating photographically the features that aid the identification and ageing of the various species. Throughout the emphasis is on identification and ageing in the field; subtle differences that may be observed on a bird in the hand are not considered.

The species covered in this book either breed in eastern N America or W Europe or occur reasonably frequently as migrants in these areas. (Many European species also occur widely, in some cases primarily, in Asia or, particularly outside the breeding season, in Africa; since this book covers only the N Atlantic area, however, these are treated simply as European.) This selection has the advantage that the shorebird enthusiast on both sides of the Atlantic is provided with reference material relating not only to his or her common species, but also to most of the vagrants or potential vagrants that originate from the other side of the Atlantic. An additional six species, and one subspecies, that are uncommon or are vagrants in the N Atlantic area are included for comparison, since they are very similar to some of the relatively common species. These are Black-winged Pratincole,* Pacific Golden Plover, Rufous-necked and Long-toed Stints, and Slender-billed and Long-billed Curlews; Snowy Plover, the N American subspecies of the widely distributed Kentish Plover, is also discussed. With these, photographs of 72 species are included; a few others that are scarce vagrants to the N Atlantic are covered briefly, under the heading 'Similar species'.

Typically, photographs are shown of each species in its juvenile, first-winter or adult winter (occasionally both), and adult summer plumages. Where the two sexes or different races of the same species have distinct plumages, these too are illustrated; only in a very few cases has it not proved possible to show a significant plumage. The number of photographs of any particular species depends very much on its range of plumages; in all, there is a total of 223 photographs in the species identification section (pp. 39–193). There is also a selection of photographs of shorebirds in flight.

The sequence of species and the scientific nomenclature follow those of Voous (1973)†. The English names used are those of the American Ornithologists' Union Check List (1983) for N American species, or are those suggested by the British Ornithologists' Union Records Committee (BOURC 1988) for European species; where these names represent significant changes from those in colloquial use, the more familiar name is also given. A few species that occur on both sides of the Atlantic have different names in the two continents; both names are used throughout, the European being given first.

Acknowledgements

In order to ensure that this volume remains reasonably compact, there can be no question of producing a general text on shorebirds. Nor do I feel competent to do so. There are already a number of books that deal extremely authoritatively with different aspects of their natural history. These books have an essential place on the shelves of any shorebird enthusiast's library, and have been consulted widely in the preparation of this volume; I acknowledge my considerable debt to them.

The following volumes have been consulted so frequently that space does not permit a detailed reference each time I have quoted from them; I hope that their respective authors will understand and forgive any liberties I may have taken. Volume 3 of *The Birds of the Western Palearctic* by Cramp & Simmons (1983) covers the shorebirds; I am

---

* Scientific names are given in the relevant species description.
† For convenience, Jack and Common Snipes have been interchanged.

particularly indebted to the accurate and detailed plumage and moult sections of this classic. The authoritative identification guide is _Shorebirds_ by Hayman, Marchant & Prater (1986), complemented by Prater, Marchant & Vuorinen's _Guide to the Identification and Ageing_ of _Holarctic Waders_ (1977), which is directed towards the study of shorebirds in the hand. Last, but by no means least, the general and very readable _Waders_ by Hale (1980) provides an excellent general natural history of the various European species.

There are others that can be read with profit and enjoyment – the Nethersole-Thompsons' _Waders: their breeding, haunts and watchers_ (1986) particularly springs to mind – but the four volumes mentioned above are those which I have found to be of the greatest value in the preparation of this book, and to the authors of which I acknowledge my grateful thanks.

My gratitude also extends to those who have actively participated in the preparation of this book. Peter Grant made many comments on the text, particularly those sections relating to identification and ageing; the book would have been much the poorer without his enthusiastic encouragement. David Tomlinson and David Rosair also willingly read and improved sections of the text. In addition, I thank Peter Holden for providing the wing-span measurements of many shorebirds.

I must, however, direct my greatest thanks in two other directions: first to the photographers who have allowed me to use their work, which is central to the book. Only infinite resources of time and travel would enable an individual to photograph all the shorebirds covered here, in all their plumages; regretfully, this is not possible. Consequently, I am very grateful to those who have both generously provided photographs and also suggested where I might find shots they have been unable to supply. I hope that they will approve of the use that has been made of their photographs.

Second, none of this considerable assistance would have been of any avail without my wife Eunice's continuing support in many directions. Her speedy typing of illegible manuscripts, patient revisions of much-corrected drafts, her forbearance when evenings and weekends were spent with 'the book', and when so-called holidays involved her as chauffeuse and caddie to an obsessed shorebird enthusiast, can never adequately be acknowledged.

Looking to the future, I would be grateful to receive any updating information or offers of photographs that will add to this collection. Please contact me at: 2 Rusland Avenue, Orpington, Kent, UK.

Richard Chandler, March 1988

THE NORTH ATLANTIC SHOREBIRD SPECIES

Shorebirds (the Charadrii) are a suborder within the Charadriiformes, an order that includes the skuas, gulls, terns and auks. The Charadrii are a group of comparatively closely related and superficially rather similar species, though they vary considerably in size; they are, however, all easily recognizable as 'shorebirds' or 'waders'. They can be subdivided into families, and these more closely related groups of species often share many characteristics, such as similarity in shape, plumage types, behaviour, and feeding methods. It is therefore convenient to introduce the N Atlantic shorebirds by discussing each species in the context of the various groups or families.

Evolution has equipped each species to take advantage of different foods available in its particular environment, and this has had an important influence on the basic features of each family, and of individual species. Those that take food at or near the surface of the ground have generally evolved as short-billed species, while those with long bills (which are often also those with long legs) probe deeply, and frequently feed in quite deep water. The food sources that shorebirds exploit vary seasonally, so that they have to move when supplies run short: a factor that has played a part in the evolution of the migratory habits of shorebirds.

Shorebirds include some of the most migratory of the world's birds. The most extreme examples are the species that exploit the abundant food supplies provided by the brief arctic summer by breeding in the high Arctic before moving south, leaving the northern winter for the southern hemisphere summer, sometimes flying to the far south of S America, S Africa or Australasia. For example, the N American White-rumped Sandpiper breeds in N Alaska and N Canada, and migrates to winter in southern S America; the Curlew Sandpiper breeds in the far north of the USSR and winters as far south as S Africa, Australia and New Zealand. The distances both of these species travel to reach their wintering grounds – and several other species could equally well have been chosen as examples – may thus be as much as 13,000 km (8000 miles).

It is the migratory behaviour of shorebirds that results in the occurrence of so many species in each of the countries around the N Atlantic. Britain, for example, has no more than about 12 which can in any sense be described as common breeding species, but a further eight species breed regularly, though with no more than about 100 or so pairs in each case. To this total may be added a further ten which occur regularly and quite commonly either as migrants on passage or as wintering birds. Additionally, in a typical year, one or more individuals of perhaps 25 further species will occur as vagrants, bringing the annual total to about 55. Comparative numbers in eastern N America are about 38 breeding and regular migrant species, which rise to perhaps 48 when vagrants are included.

Oystercatchers, stilts and avocets

The oystercatchers, stilts and avocets are comparatively closely related; all have striking black and white plumage. The two N Atlantic oystercatchers, Northern Pied and American, are both similar stockily built, noisy shorebirds with long, laterally compressed orange bills and short legs. Their toes are slightly webbed. They are predators of shellfish, and consequently their robust bills have evolved to remove molluscs from rocks and to open bivalves. The ability to do this takes some time to develop, and as a result oystercatchers are unusual among shorebirds in that they feed their young, sometimes for up to two to three months after hatching.

There is a tendency, particularly for younger birds that perhaps have still to perfect their mollusc-hunting abilities, to feed by probing in muddy strata. The bill shape of different individuals reflects this, being pointed in probers and chisel-tipped in the case of the shellfish feeders.

The acquisition of a white half-collar on the foreneck by immature and winter adult Northern Pied Oystercatchers is unique among the world's oystercatchers; all others, including the American Oyster-catcher, have similar plumages the year round after their first summer. The adult bare-part coloration, however, is not fully developed until at least the third summer and, as might be expected, breeding is thus delayed at least until then. This is a longer period of immaturity than that of any other N Atlantic shorebird.

Stilts and avocets are large, with long necks, fine pointed bills and long (avocets) or very long (stilts) legs. In the N Atlantic area there are two species of avocet and one stilt, though there are two distinctive races of the latter. While the stilts have straight bills, avocets have bills that are strongly upturned. Female avocets of both the Pied and the American species have bills that are both more strongly upcurved and shorter than that of the male. The latter feature is unique to avocets among N Atlantic shorebirds; in all other species (except those such as Ruff in which males are bigger in all dimensions than females), either both sexes have similar bill lengths or the female has the longer bill. All three species have some webbing between the toes, but only the avocets have a hind toe, and this is vestigial.

The delicate, pointed bill of the stilts has evolved for picking food, principally aquatic insects, from or from below the water surface or, less frequently, from vegetation or the ground. In contrast, the upturned bill of the avocet is flattened and rather broader at the base, though pointed at the tip; internally it has a finely lamellated structure that serves to filter small organisms from the water as the bird feeds, scything its bill from side to side in water or liquid mud.

All three species attain full adult plumage in their second winter and will often breed in their second summer. The stilts show only slight plumage differences between winter and summer, as does the Pied Avocet, but the American Avocet develops a striking cinnamon head and neck in summer plumage.

Thick-knees and pratincoles

The Northern Thick-knee or Stone-curlew is the only N Atlantic representative of the family Burhinidae, a group of large, bulky, generally brown shorebirds with proportionately large heads, large eyes and short bills. Their plumages are very similar at all ages, and they lack a hind toe. Northern Thick-knees are birds of open, often stony ground, usually occurring away from water, and are nocturnal feeders. Their food is largely earthworms and insects, though they will also take land snails and small vertebrates. Easily overlooked during the day as they are well camouflaged by their cryptic plumage, they spend considerable periods standing in a hunched posture or perhaps squatting on their tarsi. They are noisy at night – particularly on moonlit nights – during the breeding season. Outside the breeding season, particularly in autumn, they gather into flocks, though only the more northerly section of the population is migratory. Sadly, because of habitat losses, this is a declining species.

Pratincoles are medium-sized, with short bills and short legs. They are unusual as they are particularly aerial, and in flight, with their forked tails, they resemble terns or swallows. They have a well-developed hind toe, and the front three toes are partially webbed. Only one species, the Collared Pratincole, occurs regularly in the N Atlantic, breeding primarily in Spain. A very similar species, the Black-winged Pratincole, occurs as a vagrant in W Europe. It is possible that the two are races of the same species.

Pratincoles are insectivorous, usually catching their prey on the wing, though they may also feed on the ground. A gregarious family, they generally breed in loose colonies, and occur in flocks outside the breeding season. The pratincoles are unusual among the shorebirds in having a complete post-juvenile moult, so that in the field it is impossible to distinguish between first-winter and adult winter plumages.

No individuals of either the Northern Thick-knee or the pratincoles have yet wandered to N America.

Ringed-plovers

The small ringed-plovers form a group of very similar species, seven of which occur in the N Atlantic area. Four are essentially N American (Semipalmated, Wilson's and Piping Plovers; Killdeer), two are primarily European (Little Ringed and Ringed Plovers), while the Kentish/Snowy Plover occurs on both sides of the N Atlantic. These are rather dumpy, short-necked, shortish-legged and short-billed shorebirds, all of which have a white collar across the hindneck. In six of the species, the lower margin of this collar extends around the upper breast as a complete (or almost complete) dark band, the exception being the Kentish/Snowy Plover, whose breast-band is limited to patches at the sides of the neck. The Killdeer, the largest of the group, is unique in the N Atlantic area in having two black breast-bands.

The ringed-plovers are generally birds of the water's edge, particularly outside the breeding season, when most species are to be found on open sandy or muddy shores. The Killdeer, ecologically the N American equivalent of the Northern Lapwing of Europe, also occurs on open grassland. They all share the 'stop-start' feeding characteristics of the larger plovers and lapwings, intermittently standing motionless and then abruptly moving a few steps in a random direction before tilting forward, picking from the ground or water surface. The smaller plovers, however, tend to be the rather more active when feeding. On soft mud, all plovers will not infrequently use the 'foot-trembling' method, in which one foot is vibrated rapidly for several seconds. This may have the effect of temporarily liquefying the mud, causing food items to float to the surface.

All seven N Atlantic species lack a hind toe, and all except Kentish/Snowy have at least some webbing between their toes. As would be expected from its name, the Semipalmated Plover has quite extensive palmations between all three toes. If this webbing can be seen, it provides a useful distinction from the otherwise very similar Ringed Plover.

The sequence of plumages is similar in all seven species. The juvenile's upper parts are characteristically lightly scalloped, the feathers having thin dark submarginal lines and pale fringes. In first-winter plumage the juvenile mantle and scapulars are replaced with much plainer adult feathers, as are many of the more visible coverts on the folded wing. Thus, from about December onwards, it is not usually possible to distinguish first-winter from adult winter birds. The breast-bands of juvenile and winter ringed-plovers are less dark than those of summer birds, and may sometimes be incomplete. In summer plumage, females typically have brown feathers mixed in with the black areas of the head and in the breast-band. Many individuals acquire their summer plumage quite early in the year, occasionally in February, and retain it until well into October.

All seven species are migratory to a greater or lesser extent. The Ringed Plover is a 'leap-frog' migrant; the northern races winter further south than do the more southerly breeding birds, some of which are more or less sedentary. The small Canadian population and birds from Greenland probably winter in W Africa, while some British birds are thought to be resident the year round. The closely related N American Semipalmated Plover is also migratory, but several of the other N American species are less so, Piping and particularly Wilson's Plovers moving only comparatively short distances to their wintering areas. The Killdeer is unusual in being occasionally carried north in winter storms; this may explain why, as a vagrant, it occurs in Europe most often at this time, in contrast to other N American shorebird species vagrant to Europe, which are usually seen there during August–October.

The larger plovers

Six of the larger plover species, like the ringed-plovers members of the family Charadriidae, are covered here: Mountain Dotterel; European, American and Pacific Golden Plovers; Grey/Black-bellied Plover; and Northern Lapwing. Pacific Golden Plover is only a vagrant in the N Atlantic area, but is included for comparison with the closely similar American Golden Plover.

The larger plovers share many of the characters of the ringed-plovers, though they tend to be less compact, with longer necks, and are more attenuated at the rear. All have short bills and, apart from the Northern Lapwing with its characteristic crest, all have rounded heads. Moreover, they share the start-stop-tilt feeding style of the smaller plovers.

The moult sequences of the larger plovers are unexceptional, following those of typical shorebirds. In juvenile plumage, both the Mountain Dotterel and the Northern Lapwing have neat pale fringes to the upperparts and wing-covert feathers. Though in both species the winter plumage is quite similar to that of the juvenile, ageing is usually possible.

In contrast, the four *Pluvialis* plovers (three golden plovers and Grey/Black-bellied) all have finely spotted or 'spangled' upperparts as juveniles, and in the case of the three golden plovers have very similar first-winter and adult winter plumages. Ageing of these last three species is difficult, but the juveniles of all three have a characteristic mottled (in fact spotted or barred) breast and belly. Grey/Black-bellied Plovers are more easily aged since the winter upperpart feathers are paler and duller than on the juvenile, barred rather than spangled. Retained juvenile upperpart feathers allow the younger birds to be aged.

European Golden Plover
juvenile The edge-spotting ('spangling') of the upperparts, tertials and wing-coverts is distinctive of the *Pluvialis* plovers. SW England, early September. *RJC*

14

The Mountain Dotterel attains a bright summer plumage with a dark belly; unusually, the female has the brighter plumage, this reflecting the reversed breeding roles of this species in which the male is responsible for incubation, its duller plumage presumably acting as camouflage at this time. In adult summer plumage, the *Pluvialis* plovers all have a striking black face, throat, breast and belly. The summer Northern Lapwing has an increased amount of black on chin and throat, the broad black breast-band of winter plumage extending upwards.

All six species are migratory, the American and Pacific Golden Plovers flying great distances, breeding in the Arctic and wintering in S America (American Golden Plover) or in the S Pacific (Pacific Golden Plover). The Grey/Black-bellied Plover as a non-breeding bird is probably rivalled only by the Sanderling and Ruddy Turnstone as one of the most widespread of all shorebirds, for it occurs around coasts of every continent except the far south and Antarctica.

Though the Northern Lapwing does not move so far south in the winter months as the *Pluvialis* plovers, it undertakes substantial cold-weather movements, moving from continental Europe both southwest to Britain and Ireland and south to the Mediterranean and N Africa during periods of adverse weather. It is at these times that small flocks of Northern Lapwings have crossed the Atlantic to reach E Canada.

Calidris *and related sandpipers*

These shorebirds, part of a larger group often referred to as sandpipers, are composed of 15 *Calidris* and four closely allied species, the latter being the Broad-billed, Stilt and Buff-breasted Sandpipers, and the Ruff. Without exception, all are arctic-breeding species, though some, notably Dunlin and Ruff, have breeding ranges that extend southwards into the temperate zone.

As a group they are rather variable in size, Red Knot and Ruff being best described as 'medium-sized', though many are small, and they include the world's smallest shorebird, the Least Sandpiper. They have longish necks, short to medium-length bills which are often slightly decurved, and short to medium-length legs. Most feed at the water's edge, or on estuarine mudflats, sometimes wading, and pick or probe to shallow depths; the major exception is the N American Buff-breasted Sandpiper, a 'picker' which prefers a short-grass habitat.

In many of the species the sexes are generally similar, but in a few (e.g. Red Knot, Sanderling, Curlew Sandpiper and Dunlin) they differ slightly in adult summer plumage, while three species (Pectoral and Buff-breasted Sandpipers and Ruff) show considerable sexual dimorphism, in each case the male being the larger. Moreover, the

Semipalmated Sandpiper

juvenile One of the group of small *Calidris* sandpipers, showing characteristic neat, pale-fringed juvenile upperpart feathers. New York, mid-September. *RJC*

male Ruff is the only shorebird to develop the elongate neck feathers which give it its English name. This species is also unusual in that both sexes (though particularly the male) have a wide range of coloration in adult summer plumage.

The smallest *Calidris* species (colloquially 'stints' or 'peeps') are very similar to each other, and provide some of the most difficult of all identification problems. This is particularly so with the three species pairs: Semipalmated and Western Sandpipers of N America (which alone in the group have partially webbed feet); Little and Rufous-necked Stints of Europe and Asia respectively; and Least Sandpiper (N America) and Long-toed Stint (Asia).

The plumage sequence is generally similar for all the species in the group, but, although many attain full breeding plumages (and indeed breed) in their first summer, others do not and acquire only an incomplete version of their breeding plumage. Frequently, the juvenile plumage is comparatively brightly coloured and is not unlike that of the adult summer bird; Dunlin is a good example of this. Exceptions to this are those species which develop strong underpart colours in breeding plumage, e.g. Red Knot, Curlew Sandpiper and Stilt Sandpiper. First-winter birds often retain at least some of their worn juvenile feathers, which usually allow them to be distinguished from the more uniformly coloured (and patterned) adult winter individuals.

As arctic-breeding species these are all migrants, and include some of the world's most far-travelled birds. Several of the N American species, particularly Pectoral Sandpiper and Buff-breasted Sandpiper, have a southward migration route that takes a proportion of their populations over the W Atlantic. It is not surprising that these two species, displaced eastwards by tropical storms, are among the most frequent N American vagrants to Europe.

Snipes, dowitchers and woodcocks

All seven N Atlantic species in this group have in common a long or very long, straight bill, and feed by continually probing deep into soft mud with a 'sewing-machine' action. As with many shorebirds, their bill tips are not only sensitive but also have some flexibility, aiding the detection and capture of prey at depth. This flexibility relates mainly to the upper mandible and is well shown by the Common Snipe below.

In spite of the currently accepted sequence of species (Voous 1973), which places the dowitchers between the snipes and the woodcocks, most field observers will agree that the snipes and woodcocks together share a number of characteristics, and that the two dowitchers of N America are rather different.

The snipes and woodcocks are chunky, small or medium-sized shorebirds, with short or very short legs. They generally appear short-necked, but Common and Great Snipes are in fact fairly long-necked, a feature they may show when alarmed. All have cryptic brown plumage which varies a little (Common and Great Snipes) or not at all (Jack Snipe, woodcocks) with age or season. Consequently, though the larger two snipes can with care and close views sometimes be aged, this is impossible with the other three species. Nor can the sexes of any of the snipes or woodcocks be separated.

The woodcocks are generally nocturnal feeders. They also share with the Common Snipe the unusual habit for shorebirds of feeding their young, though only while they are quite small.

In contrast to the snipes and woodcocks, the two dowitchers, which are medium-sized with medium-length legs, are fairly long-necked and are slightly less compact. Females of both dowitcher species have

Common Snipe
adult Showing
the flexibility of the
upper mandible.
E England, mid-
September. *RJC*

longer bills than the males, but, since bill lengths overlap considerably, only the shortest-billed male Short-billed and the longest-billed female Long-billed can be safely identified on this character alone. Again, in contrast to the other species in this group, the dowitchers have distinctive juvenile, winter and summer plumages, and thus can be aged without undue difficulty. The two species are, however, very similar to one another in adult winter and adult summer plumages, and here great care is required in making a specific identification, especially in winter plumage. In summer plumage, like the godwits which in many respects they resemble closely, they develop brick-red head and underparts.

All the seven species are migratory, though some populations of the Common Snipe, particularly in the southern parts of its range, are perhaps sedentary; a similar situation exists with the American Woodcock. It is of interest that some Long-billed Dowitchers, which in N America breed only in Alaska and far NW Canada, migrate southeast across Canada to the Atlantic seaboard. It is presumably some of these individuals, blown eastwards across the Atlantic, that appear annually as vagrants in Europe. Short-billed Dowitchers, though, are virtually unknown in Europe, suggesting that their migration route is overland or near coastal and rarely takes them out over the Atlantic to be blown off course.

Godwits, curlews and Upland Sandpiper

The godwits and curlews are large to very large shorebirds, with long bills which are straight, or nearly so, in the case of the godwits and strongly decurved in the curlews. All the world's four godwits (Black- and Bar-tailed in Europe, Hudsonian and Marbled in N America) and four of its eight curlews (Western and Slender-billed in Europe, Long- billed in N America, and Whimbrel in both continents) occur in the N Atlantic area. The Upland Sandpiper is smaller, medium-sized, with a short bill. The godwits are not dissimilar to the dowitchers, and (apart from Marbled Godwit) share with them distinctive juvenile and winter plumages, and brick-red underparts in summer plumage. The Marbled Godwit has a barred cinnamon plumage at all ages. The curlews have generally brown, barred plumage, again very similar at all ages, though the juveniles can, with care, be separated from adults. In most of the species the female is marginally larger, often duller, but with a noticeably longer bill than the male.

All these long-billed shorebirds feed by wading or by deep probing in soft mud. Outside the breeding season the Black-tailed and Hudsonian Godwits prefer fresh water, while the other godwits and all the curlew species usually occur on coasts or estuaries.

Bar-tailed Godwit
juvenile Juvenile godwits and curlews have more strongly patterned tertials (which lie just above the folded wing-tips) than do the adults; in this species they are strongly edge-spotted. SW England, early September. *RJC*

The Upland Sandpiper has a curlew-like barred brown plumage nearly similar the year round. It differs from the other species in the group in being an inland, grassland bird with a general behaviour pattern reminiscent of the larger plovers.

All the species are migratory, but the ranges of the Marbled Godwit and the Long-billed Curlew are largely contained within N America, and perhaps because of this these two have not occurred in Europe. The European race of the Whimbrel has not been seen in N America, but the other species (and the N American race of Whimbrel) have all appeared as vagrants on the opposite side of the N Atlantic to that where they breed. The Slender-billed Curlew is a very rare vagrant to W Europe which breeds in only small numbers in central USSR and winters in N Africa.

Tringa *and related sandpipers*

Nine *Tringa* sandpipers are regular in the N Atlantic area; six are European, the remainder American in origin. All have occurred in W Europe, but three of the European species (Common Redshank, Marsh Sandpiper and Green Sandpiper) have not yet been seen in eastern N America. They are elegant, delicately built, small or medium-sized shorebirds with medium-length to long, generally straight bills, long necks, and medium-length to long legs. All have hind toes and a limited amount of webbing between the toes. These features are also shared by the two small *Actitis* sandpipers, Common and Spotted, of Europe and America respectively. Spotted Sandpiper occurs as a vagrant in Europe, and has bred once in Britain.

All are found largely by fresh water, where they feed at the water's edge or by wading. The larger species may wade quite deeply, and all can occasionally be seen swimming. Most will also use coastal localities, particularly outside the breeding season.

A characteristic feature of many *Tringa*, but especially the smaller ones and also the two *Actitis* species, is their habit of bobbing or 'teetering'. Particularly when disturbed, they bob on flexed legs, wagging their tails with an up-and-down motion.

In discussing the plumages of these sandpipers it is convenient to consider them in four groups: Spotted Redshank; the larger *Tringa*; the smaller *Tringa* sandpipers; and the *Actitis* sandpipers. The Spotted Redshank, like the other larger species, has strongly spotted upperparts in juvenile plumage and is relatively uniformly greyish above in winter. Unlike the other species, however, the juvenile Spotted Redshank has irregularly barred underparts, and the summer adult acquires a very distinctive, completely black, head and body. The other larger *Tringa* have less obviously distinctively adult summer plumages, typically acquiring darker upperparts and tertials (often with a scattering of adult winter-type feathers) and fairly heavily streaked underparts. All retain juvenile wing-coverts in their first-winter plumage.

The smaller *Tringa* sandpipers (Solitary, Green and Wood Sandpipers) have rather similar plumages at all ages. All have dark brownish upperparts with pale-spotted feather edges, Wood Sandpiper having generally the larger spots of the three species. In juvenile and adult summer plumages all three are more brightly spotted, with larger, whiter spots than in winter, and in their first-winter all retain many juvenile wing-coverts. Their general coloration, however, is such that these worn feathers are by no means easy to observe in the field, and it can prove difficult to age many individuals.

Lesser Yellowlegs
juvenile Juvenile *Tringa* sandpipers have strongly edge-spotted upperparts, wing-coverts and tertials. New York, late September. *RJC*

The Common and Spotted Sandpipers, closely related and, except in adult summer plumage, very similar to each other, are the smallest of the group. In general coloration they both resemble the smaller *Tringa* sandpipers, and, although all have distinctive juvenile plumages, their various winter and summer plumages are all very similar. The exception is the adult summer Spotted Sandpiper, which acquires distinctive boldly spotted underparts.

All the species in the group breed in wetlands or near the water's edge; they favour the more northerly temperate regions or the low Arctic. All are migratory, though the more southerly breeding birds of some of the species (notably Common Redshank) are only short-distance migrants or are sedentary.

Willet, Ruddy Turnstone and the phalaropes

These are a group of disparate species. The Willet is a large *Tringa*-like American shorebird with a fairly heavy, medium-length straight bill and long grey legs. It has partially webbed feet. Its juvenile, winter and summer plumages are all distinctive; the most notable feature is its striking black and white wing pattern, unexpected until it takes flight. The Willet breeds in saltmarshes and prairie wetlands, and outside the breeding season is found in a variety of generally coastal habitats. There are two or three records from the eastern side of the Atlantic.

The Ruddy Turnstone, though a breeding bird of the high Arctic, is one of the most widespread of all shorebird species, occurring nearly world-wide around the coasts. As its name suggests, it frequently feeds by turning stones, seaweed and other debris with its bill as it searches for food. It has distinctive juvenile, winter and adult summer plumages and may usually be aged easily.

There are three species of phalarope, all of which occur on both sides of the Atlantic, though Wilson's Phalarope is a N American species which occurs in Europe only as a vagrant. Wilson's also differs from the Red-necked and Grey/Red Phalaropes in its more temperate inland-wetland breeding habitat, the other two being arctic or high-arctic breeding birds, and in wintering in inland wetlands (in S America). In contrast, the Red-necked and Grey/Red Phalaropes winter at sea, and are the only pelagic shorebirds: in the Atlantic, Grey/Red winters far offshore off W Africa, while both species winter in the Pacific off S America.

All three phalaropes are small or medium-sized, relatively long-necked, and have medium-length or short straight bills, and shortish legs. The Grey/Red Phalarope's short bill is flattened and surprisingly broad, but the two other species have needle-fine bills. All have

Red-necked Phalarope
juvenile Feeding while swimming, in typical phalarope manner. California, mid-September. *RJC*

partially webbed and lobed feet for swimming. Though Wilson's feeding behaviour often resembles that of other shorebirds in that it picks from the ground surface or wades, on occasion it shares the Red-necked and Grey/Red Phalaropes' characteristic style of feeding while swimming, spinning to stir up food items from the water.

All the phalaropes have distinct juvenile, winter and summer plumages. Like the Mountain Dotterel, they have reversed sexual roles, the male incubating and caring for the chicks. The adult summer plumages reflect this behaviour, the females being the more brightly coloured.

Grey/Red Phalaropes move south to their offshore southern hemisphere wintering areas by travelling far out to sea. Consequently 'wrecks' of storm-blown birds occur inland from time to time on both sides of the Atlantic. A similar situation exists with the Red-necked Phalarope off N America, but in Europe this species migrates south or even southeast overland to winter in the Arabian Sea, and so is uncommon in W Europe. Wilson's Phalarope is generally an inland migrant in N America, and is not particularly common along the coast.

SHOREBIRD PLUMAGES
AND MOULTS

Deciding the age of a shorebird – and sometimes also the initial identification – often depends on an ability to recognize the different patterns presented by particular groups of feathers. Knowledge is thus required of the names and locations of the various feather groups on a bird. Additionally, since the patterns on the feathers change both with the age of the bird and with the seasons, the observer should also be aware of the timing and sequence in which the birds moult their feathers.

Plumage terminology

The main feather groups which are of value for identification and ageing in the field are those that are visible when the bird is standing, and these are illustrated by the Purple Sandpiper in the Frontispiece. Terminology for other parts of the body (the 'bare parts') is also given. The terms used here follow those adopted by the journal *British Birds* (1981); the more important feather groups are given in Table 1.

It can be convenient when describing bird plumages to lump together some of the feather groups, and the terms 'face', 'neck' and 'flight feathers' as indicated in Table 1 are used in this book. With standing shorebirds, frequently the mantle and scapulars are all that can be seen of the upperparts, and these two groups of feathers are often referred to together as 'upperparts' in the species descriptions.

It will be seen in the Frontispiece that the wing-coverts are partly obscured by the scapulars. This occurs particularly with adult shorebirds, which generally have rather larger scapulars (and other body feathers) than the smaller, neater, feathers of the juvenile. Compare, for example, the juvenile and adult Ruffs shown on pp. 129 and 131.

The relative positions of the feather groups on the wing are best seen when shorebirds extend their wings: sometimes stretching sideways one wing at a time (wing-stretching, Fig. 1), sometimes raising both wings vertically (wing-lifting, Fig. 2). These figures show the separation of the flight feathers into the primaries on the outer wing, and the secondaries and tertials on the inner wing. It can be seen, too, that the wing-coverts visible on the folded wing of a standing shorebird are the greater,

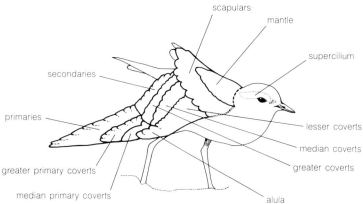

Fig. 1. Mountain Dotterel *juvenile*, wing-stretching, showing feather groups on wing; the tertials are hidden beneath the scapulars.
SW England, early September. *RJC*
(The inset shows features of the flight pattern)

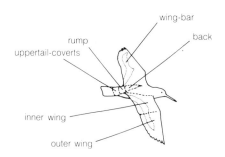

Table 1. Principal feather groups used in this book

General area	Feather groups		
Head and neck	Forehead	Chin and throat	⎤
	Crown	Lores	⎬ 'face'
	Nape	Ear-coverts	⎦
	Hindneck; sides of neck; foreneck ('neck')		
Upperparts	Mantle	Rump	
	Scapulars	Uppertail-coverts	
	Back		
Underparts	Chin and throat	Flanks	
	Breast	Vent	
	Belly	Undertail-coverts	
Wings	Primaries	⎤	
	Secondaries	⎬ 'flight feathers'	
	Tertials	⎦	
Upperwing	Greater coverts	⎤	
	Median coverts	⎬ 'inner wing-coverts'	
	Lesser coverts	⎦	
	Greater primary coverts	⎤	
	Median primary coverts	⎬ 'outer wing-coverts'	
	Lesser primary coverts	⎦	
	Alula		
Underwing	Greater underwing-coverts	⎤	
	Median underwing-coverts	⎬ 'underwing-coverts'	
	Lesser underwing-coverts	⎦	
	Axillaries		
Tail	Tail		

Fig. 2. Green Sandpiper *adult summer*, wing-lifting; the tertials are the longer, pointed feathers at the base of the wing, and the delicately striped feathers are the axillaries. This individual is in wing moult. E England, early July. *RJC*

25

median and lesser coverts, together the 'inner wing-coverts'. Corresponding feather groups exist beneath the wing: the 'underwing-coverts', Fig. 2. The group of feathers at the base of the underwing where it joins the body, the axillaries, is important in the identification of Grey/Black-bellied Plover and golden plovers.

All shorebirds have 11 primaries, but the outermost is tiny, virtually one of the covert feathers. The number of secondaries varies with the size of the bird; the smaller species, for example Curlew Sandpiper and Red-necked Phalarope, typically have ten, whereas the largest species such as the Western Curlew can have up to 21. The tertials (the flight feathers nearest the body) are secondaries modified to cover and protect the true secondaries, and are usually clearly visible on a standing shorebird, overlying and concealing the secondaries.

Plumage marks

Areas of distinctively coloured feathers or parts of feathers also often provide useful field marks. These are not feather groups as listed in Table 1, but are none the less invaluable for plumage descriptions. Those used in this book are as follows. *Supercilium* is the pale stripe immediately above the eye; *eye-stripe* is the dark stripe through the eye (shown, for example, by the dowitchers, pp. 138 and 139); *crown-stripe* is the pale stripe running through the centre of the crown; *wing-bar* is the white or pale bar along part or all of the length of the wing shown by many shorebirds when wing-stretching or in flight. The *wing-bar* is usually formed by the pale tips of the greater coverts or by adjacent white areas on the primaries. The *shoulder-patch* of some species is formed by an area of contrastingly darker lesser coverts, and is often particularly obvious at the bend of the folded wing on standing birds; these dark feathers also show in flight, emphasizing the wing pattern. Sanderling, particularly in winter plumage, and Broad-billed Sandpiper are examples of species showing shoulder-patches.

*Mantle V*s and/or *scapular V*s are formed by the juxtaposition of the pale margins of mantle and scapular feathers, and are shown particularly by juveniles of such species as Little Stint and Pectoral Sandpiper.

Feather patterns and wear

The individual feathers may be plain (as they are on many shorebirds in winter), or patterned. The patterning may be simple and easily described, but may also be extremely complex. As with the different feather groups, a standard terminology, such as that developed by Prater *et al.* (1977) and extended by Hayman *et al.* (1986), is useful. The terms used here to describe feather patterns are given in Fig. 3.

Fig. 3. Feather patterns and feather wear

Fringed, with dark subterminal line | Barred | Edge-spotted | Notched | Notched, and worn

All the feathers on a bird's plumage wear with time, but exposed feathers, particularly those on the upperparts, the inner wing-coverts, the tertials and the tips of the longest primaries, are affected more. Fresh, new feathers have rounded tips and neat edges, but as time progresses the tips at first appear frayed and slightly irregular, and eventually may become quite pointed. The sides of the feathers also wear, but this is usually less apparent except where the feather has a notched or spotted pattern. In these latter cases the wear is greater on the paler parts of the feather, often resulting in the sides of the feather having a very irregular profile; see Fig. 3. Feather fringes may be lost in a similar manner.

Bare parts

The unfeathered parts of the bird – the 'bare parts' – though obviously not part of the plumage proper, are treated in this section since their colours are also of value for identification and ageing. This applies particularly to the bill and legs, and in some species to the eye, where the colour of the iris and the orbital ring may be useful. The orbital ring should not be confused with the eye-ring: the orbital ring is the bare skin immediately surrounding the eye, whereas the eye-ring is a ring of tiny feathers immediately surrounding the orbital ring. Similar feathers also cover the eyelids, so that a species with a pale eye-ring usually has pale eyelids, which can be conspicuous when it is roosting; see the Short-billed Dowitcher, Fig. 4.

A coating of mud on bill or legs can obscure their natural colours and thus must always be kept in mind. Less well appreciated is the possibility that the bare parts may be stained, with consequent long-term discoloration. Such staining is not very common; but white discoloration can occur where birds have been feeding in calcareous or other alkaline environments, and this can affect both bill and legs. The adult summer Northern Pied Oystercatcher (p. 43) shows slight staining of this type on its bill, while the adult summer Curlew Sandpiper (p. 115) shows extreme white staining, almost an encrustation, on its black bill and legs. Brownish staining from water with a high iron content also occurs, and may perhaps explain the atypical leg colour of the first-winter Bar-tailed Godwit (p. 149).

Seasonal plumage changes

Shorebirds have a succession of different plumages that change with the age of the individual and with the seasons. A number of different terminologies have been used to define the various plumages and also the intervening moults. The *British Birds* (1985) nomenclature is used here, and is compared in Table 2 with the terminology devised by Humphrey & Parkes (1959), which is widely used in N America. I do not intend to give a complete account of the moult of shorebirds, which is covered well by Hale (1980) and by Ginn & Melville (1983). My purpose is simply to discuss those aspects of the moult that aid the ageing of the various species in the field.

On hatching, the chick has a fluffy downy plumage. This is quickly replaced, usually within the first three weeks, by the first set of true feathers, which form the *juvenile* plumage. These feathers grow as a continuation of the down, which is carried on the tips of the true feathers. The down soon falls or wears off, though occasionally, as with the Northern Thick-knee and the *Charadrius* plovers, tail-down may be retained for a week or so after the bird has attained its complete juvenile plumage; see the juvenile Little Ringed Plover, p.58. Fig. 5 shows a young juvenile Common Redshank that still retains some down, both on the nape and on the tail. Although this newly fledged individual can probably fly, its feathers, particularly its flight feathers, are still growing, giving it a rather short rear end; compare its overall profile with that of the apparently longer-bodied full-grown juvenile of the same species shown on p. 163, which also has a longer bill. There is a tendency for bill growth to continue in otherwise full-grown juveniles, as can often be seen with the larger and long-billed shorebirds: juvenile curlews often have noticeably shorter bills than adults.

Fig. 4. Short-billed Dowitcher *first-winter*, roosting; note the worn wing-coverts, the white-feathered lower eyelid, and the diagnostic 'tiger-striped' tertial retained from its juvenile plumage. Florida, mid-January. *RJC*

Thus, within a few weeks of hatching (about three weeks for some of the smaller species, up to six for the larger), the bird has its first complete set of true feathers and can fly. The characteristic patterns of these juvenile feathers, particularly those of the upperparts, are often quite similar within closely related groups of species. The small *Calidris* sandpipers generally have neat pale fringes to their upperpart feathers, while the corresponding feathers on juvenile *Tringa* shorebirds are strongly spotted. These plumage similarities among groups of shorebirds have been discussed in the first chapter.

Table 2. Terminology and timing of plumages and moults of N Atlantic shorebirds. The *British Birds* terminology is used in this book; the names of moults are in italic (after *British Birds* 1985; Hale 1980)

British Birds	*Humphrey & Parkes (1959)*	*Usual plumage or moult period*
Juvenile	Juvenile	May–September
Moult to first-winter or *post-juvenile moult*	*First prebasic moult*	August–November
First-winter	First basic	October–April
Moult to first-summer	*First prealternate moult*	February–May
First-summer	First alternate	February–September
Moult to adult winter	*Prebasic moult*	July–November
Adult winter	Definitive basic	October–April
Moult to adult summer	*Prealternate moult*	February–May
Adult summer	Definitive alternate	February–September

Fig. 5. Common Redshank *young juvenile*, still showing traces of down. E England, mid-July. RJC

The juvenile feathers are often noticeably softer than those of adults, and wear more quickly. Perhaps as a consequence of this, juveniles soon – some almost immediately after fledging – commence moult into their *first-winter* plumage. The post-juvenile moult is generally a partial one, and usually involves most of the body feathers (i.e. those of head, neck, upperparts and underparts) and a variable number of the wing-coverts and tertials; the juvenile primaries, secondaries and tail feathers are usually retained. Only coursers and pratincoles among the shorebirds replace all their feathers at the post-juvenile moult.

As a result of this moult, the appearance of most shorebirds is significantly changed. Juvenile feathers are often quite bright and fairly strongly patterned; in contrast, the newly acquired first-winter feathers are often comparatively dull and featureless, so that by the time the moult to first-winter plumage is complete (typically some time in November) the bird often appears a plainer, drabber individual.

In many instances, the first-winter bird can be distinguished from the otherwise very similar adult winter by the unmoulted (but worn) feathers retained from its juvenile plumage. The particular feather groups to examine are the wing-coverts and the tertials, though the number of these feathers that are lost at the post-juvenile moult varies between species, and also between races and individuals of the same species.

The retained feathers are often differently patterned, and will certainly be more worn than the fresh first-winter feathers of the mantle and scapulars. This is illustrated by Fig. 4, which shows the considerable contrast between the worn juvenile wing-coverts and the fresh, newly acquired mantle and scapulars of a first-winter Short-billed Dowitcher. In comparison, an adult winter bird at the same season has fairly fresh, unworn feathers on both upperparts and wing-coverts, as shown on p. 138.

Not all first-winter shorebirds are so easy to age as the individual in Fig. 4. A number of species lose most of their juvenile wing-coverts during the post-juvenile moult, and gain feathers similar to those of the winter adult; examples are the pratincoles and Common Snipe. Alternatively, they have, as juveniles, feathers that are already very similar to those of adult winter birds and which they retain in their first-winter plumage, as is the case with Common and Spotted Sandpipers. Under these circumstances, ageing of shorebirds in winter plumage becomes difficult, and sometimes impossible, particularly in the field. A further category where ageing is difficult arises in a few species in which the plumages are identical at all ages; Jack Snipe and American Woodcock are the only examples of this in the N Atlantic.

In turn, the first-winter bird will moult again in spring to attain its *first-summer* plumage. Again, this is a partial moult which typically involves body feathers, some wing-coverts, and in some species a few flight feathers. It is thus comparable in its extent with the post-juvenile moult. There is, however, rather more variation among species in the extent of the moult to first-summer plumage. At this stage some species, particularly the smaller, gain a plumage virtually identical to that of summer adults. Indeed, many individuals of the smaller species will breed in their first summer. On the other hand, many (if not most) of the larger species do not normally breed in their first summer, and a good number of these individuals will remain in their wintering areas; these birds rarely attain the plumage of the adult breeding birds, but either retain first-winter plumage or gain a mixture of adult summer and winter-type plumage. Examples of first-summer birds are provided by the Common Redshank (p. 163) and the Common Greenshank (p. 167).

At their next moult most species acquire their *adult winter* plumage. An exception occurs with the oystercatchers, which take two or three years to reach maturity; even so, sub-adults can be reliably aged only on their bare-part colours, and not on their plumage, which is virtually identical to that of adults. Shorebirds are sometimes seen in adult winter plumage as early as August. These are probably non-breeding first-summer birds, which often attain their adult winter plumage before the full adults, whose moult is usually delayed until the end of their breeding season. Breeding adults do not generally attain winter plumage until October, and often later. Both first-summer and adult summer shorebirds have a complete moult, including their flight feathers, in attaining their adult winter plumage. By this time the flight feathers of the first-summer birds are upwards of 15 months old, and are often bleached and well worn before they are finally shed.

In spring the adults have a body moult and gain their breeding or *adult summer* plumage. This plumage can change noticeably during the course of the summer; many of the *Calidris* species, for example, have pale-fringed but dark-centred upperpart feathers, and thus, as the fringes wear off, the overall plumage becomes darker. Feather-darkening also occurs as a distinct colour change, perhaps resulting from oxidation, which can sometimes be seen in Common Redshanks and Common Greenshanks (Hale 1980). The same process may also affect shorebirds in their greyish winter plumage, some individuals appearing quite dark by the end of winter. Feather-bleaching can also occur, and this is most obvious with the small ringed-plovers, which in both summer and winter plumage can become noticeably paler as the feathers age.

Some species have, as breeding adults, summer-plumage upperparts that consist of a mixture of summer- and winter-type feathers, both feather types being acquired in the moult to adult summer plumage. Examples are Common Redshank and Common Greenshank, the effect being particularly obvious in the southern race (*T.t.totanus*) of the former (Hale 1980).

Primary moult

Most detailed studies of the timing and feather-by-feather sequence of moult in shorebirds have been concentrated on the flight feathers, particularly the primaries, which in all species are shed in the moult to adult winter plumage. Not a great deal is known concerning the progression of body moult related to the primary moult, except that in general the moult period of the primaries is comparable with that of the remainder of the plumage. When a bird lifts its wings, or when it is in flight, it is possible to see the extent of the moult of the flight feathers, which commences with the inner primaries, typically the first three to five being shed almost simultaneously. The remaining feathers are then lost symmetrically on both wings, the primaries in sequence towards the wing-tip and the secondaries towards the body. The Green Sandpiper in Fig. 2 has just lost the inner three primaries on each wing and shows the characteristic 'stepped' shape of the trailing edge of the wing resulting from the considerably greater length of the remaining primaries compared with the adjacent secondaries. This wing shape is usually quite obvious on moulting shorebirds seen in flight, even if a gap is not present between the primaries and secondaries.

PHOTOGRAPHING SHOREBIRDS

It is appropriate, in a book concerned mainly with photographs of shorebirds, to say something about methods and the equipment needed. I am concerned here with photography of shorebirds away from the nest, and presume a knowledge of basic photographic principles on the part of the reader. Excellent and more extensive discussion of the subject will also be found in *Natural History Photography*, edited by Turner Ettlinger (1974), *The Technique of Bird Photography* by Warham (1983), and *A Field Guide to Photographing Birds* by Hill & Langsbury (1987).

Equipment and accessories

Medium-format cameras, having a negative size of typically 6cm × 7cm, are generally inappropriate for bird photography away from the nest owing to their bulk (and therefore difficulty of handling), expense, and the lack of suitable long-focal-length lenses. The latter is important, since, to get an image comparable with that obtained with the more compact 35mm equipment (which has a negative size of 24mm × 36mm), the medium-format camera requires, for example, a cumbersome 500mm focal-length lens instead of, in 35mm format, a relatively compact 300mm lens. The 35mm format has the further advantage of the availability of a considerable range of equipment, which, because of its portability, is particularly convenient for shorebird photography. With careful technique, high-quality results can be obtained with 35mm equipment. For these reasons, 35mm equipment is generally used for shorebird photography, and with one exception (American Woodcock p. 142) all the photographs in this book were taken in this format.

The single-lens 35mm reflex camera has the advantages both of accepting interchangeable lenses and of providing the same image in the viewfinder as will appear on the negative. For the shorebird photographer the most important features required from the camera are: through-the-lens (TTL) metering; a fastest shutter speed (particularly useful for flight photography) of 1/1000 sec. or even 1/2000 sec.;

automatic exposure is useful, but this should be capable of being overridden to allow manual control of awkward lighting situations; interchangeable viewfinder screens allow the fitting of a plain screen, which is almost essential with long-focal-length lenses; and the camera body should accept a motor-drive.

Long-focal-length telephoto lenses are a basic necessity for shorebird photography, at least away from the nest. There can be no doubt that the best results are obtained with relatively short-focal-length lenses, but it is often not possible to get close enough to the subject to be able to use, say, a 135mm lens and still obtain an adequate image size on the resulting transparency or negative. In practice, the best focal-length to use is about 400mm, but 600mm lenses are increasingly popular, though those with a maximum aperture of f5.6 are heavy and bulky, and require careful handling to obtain sharp results.

There is a choice between conventional lenses and catadioptric or mirror-lens types. The advantages of the former are that generally, for the same focal-length, they have larger maximum apertures, are capable of being stopped-down to smaller apertures to improve depth of field, and they lack the unattractive circular out-of-focus highlights of the mirror lens. An example of the latter effect is seen in the photograph of the juvenile Ruff, p. 130. The mirror lens gains in being less bulky, and in being capable of closer focusing. Both types of lens are usually excellent optically.

An important aspect of lens performance for all bird photography is how close the lens will focus. Unless this is relatively close, it is impossible (other than by using inconvenient extension tubes) to get a reasonable image size of the smaller species. In practice, this distance should be not much greater than 4m (13ft) for a 400mm lens, and pro rata for other focal-lengths.

The focal-length of a lens may be increased by a converter or multiplier. The most commonly used converters increase the focal-length (and hence the image size) by a factor of either ×1.4 or ×2; these can be invaluable, but some loss of image quality is inevitable. Even though modern converters are of a high quality, their major drawback is the loss of light: one stop with the ×1.4, and two stops with the ×2 converter. This reduction in the effective aperture of the prime lens often proves to be unacceptable, particularly with the ×2 converter if a slow film is being used. This is due largely to the difficulty of avoiding camera shake, which results in a blurred image. Examples of photographs taken with a ×1.4 converter are the first-winter Northern Pied Oystercatcher (p. 43) and the winter Common Sandpiper (p. 179).

The problems of camera shake become greater with increasing focal-length; for a hand-held camera/lens combination it is recommended that, to avoid the effects of shake, the shutter speed in seconds should be equal to or less than the reciprocal of the focal-length of the lens in millimetres. Thus, an exposure time of 1/500 sec. or less should be used with a 500mm focal-length lens. If the available light or the film speed do not allow such shutter speeds, then some form of camera support is essential. A 'rifle-grip' or 'shoulder-pod' will often allow a shutter speed of 1/250 sec. or even 1/125 sec. to be used with a 400mm lens, and is especially helpful when stalking or when photographing birds in flight. A monopod, particularly when used only partly extended, can allow a shutter speed of 1/125 sec. (with care, and a little luck, 1/60 sec.) to be used, even with a heavy 600mm lens. This, again, is convenient for stalking. A reasonably heavy tripod will generally give good results with shutter speeds of 1/60 sec. whatever the focal-length of the lens, provided the camera is solidly clamped. Clearly the latter method of support is preferable, and can be used from a hide, but it is not always convenient for stalking.

Surprisingly good results are possible when hand-holding the camera, with the front end of the lens resting on a bean bag on the windowsill of a car or permanent hide, or on some other convenient support.

A motor-drive giving automatic film wind-on after each exposure can be useful, especially for flight photography, making it much easier to keep the subject in focus and allowing several shots while the bird remains within range. The noise of the motor-drive, however, may disturb the bird, particularly when the camera is used from a hide.

Film stock

Most bird photographers work with colour transparency or black and white negative film. The usual preference, given reasonable light and a maximum lens aperture of not less than, say, f5.6, is for a film speed of 64 ISO (ASA) for transparency film. In duller light, or with lenses of smaller maximum aperture (or when the effective aperture is reduced by the use of a converter), faster film with a speed of 200 or 400 ISO may be required. I prefer Kodachrome 64 (which has been used for nearly all the colour photographs in this book), or Kodachrome 200 when a higher speed film is needed. Of course, the latter carries with it the drawback of slightly less-fine grain. With black and white film, presuming that reasonably fine grain is a primary requirement, 125 ISO conventional film or 400 ISO chromogenic film give very similar results. My choice here is for Ilford FP4 (rated at 200 ISO, and developed in Patterson's Aculux) or the chromogenic Ilford XP1. The latter requires higher-temperature development in film-specific chemicals, but in practice this does not introduce any undue difficulty.

The use of colour film has its own particular problems in correct colour rendition. Film of any one type will vary slightly from batch to batch. Colour balance is of course affected by incorrect exposure, but, even in full sunlight and when correctly exposed, the colour balance will vary during the course of the day. If required, 'warm' early-morning or evening light (seen with the winter Short-billed Dowitcher, p. 138) may be corrected using a filter (Wratten 82A). In overcast conditions, or when the subject is in shadow, the resulting picture will show a bluish cast; this can be corrected to a certain extent by the use of an 81A filter. These are the problems of the photographer; when it is also realized that in reproducing the resulting transparency for publication further difficulties arise, it will be seen that caution is needed when comparing colours of the different photographs in this (or any other) publication.

Methods of shorebird photography

Away from the nest, there are two basic types of shorebird photography: 'wait-and-see', and stalking. The former is usually practised from a small portable hide (or blind), or from a vehicle. Two situations lend themselves to the wait-and-see technique for photographing shorebirds: birds feeding, and birds at high-tide roosts. Both situations require a certain amount of fieldwork before a photographic session can be attempted.

Areas where shorebirds regularly feed have to be found, and an appropriate site for the hide must be selected. This must be located so that the light comes from behind at the intended time of occupancy; be between about five to ten or so metres from where the birds feed (depending on the focal-length of the lens to be used), and preferably set back from the feeding area among vegetation. The use of 'transplanted' vegetation or other camouflage to disguise the hide can be beneficial. If the hide can be left in place for some time, even a day or so, to allow the birds to become used to it, so much the better. Alternatively, disturbance can sometimes be minimized by erecting and occupying a hide at or before first light.

Shorebird photography at high-tide roosting sites can be rather a chancy affair, with the birds avoiding the hide unless their choice of roosting area is very restricted. Additionally, the roosting site may change with the height of the tide – which may also threaten the photographer in his hide. Nevertheless, successful roost photography can be both exciting and rewarding, with the only problem being the choice of bird to photograph. The Northern Pied Oystercatchers, p. 43, were all photographed at a high-tide roost, as was the juvenile Black-tailed Godwit, p. 144.

Fig. 6. Hide/blind for shorebird photography

A hide should be as inconspicuous as possible; it will be most easily camouflaged by making it no larger than required to accommodate the sitting photographer, together with his tripod and other equipment. To do this requires a plan area of about one metre square and a height of perhaps one and a half metres. Other requirements are 'windows' for the camera lens and for viewing, and a reasonably substantial frame to which the fabric can be attached. An example of a purpose-made hide is shown in Fig. 6: the corner poles slide into tubes of material to ensure that if it is windy the fabric cannot flap noisily against the frame; the frame is sufficiently rigid not to require guy ropes (providing it is not too windy), and the hide can be moved by the occupant should this be required during a photographic session. Alternatively, similar hides can quickly and cheaply be put together using a simple timber frame with hessian or other fabric attached with drawing pins or carpet tacks.

Shorebirds may sometimes be stalked, but this generally requires a comparatively co-operative subject. Some species are more confiding than others; Mountain Dotterels, Purple Sandpipers and the phalaropes are often quite tame. Some individuals are also more approachable than others, this applying particularly to young birds and tired migrants. The latter should not be harassed, but allowed to feed or roost; the welfare of the bird is more important than the photograph. The approachability of shorebirds also depends on geographical location; I have found them to be more easily photographed in N America and in Africa than in Europe.

The key to successful stalking lies in a slow, careful approach to the bird. Keep low if possible, and avoid sudden movements. Make use of even small topographic or vegetational features to separate you from the bird; a short stretch of water can often be surprisingly useful. I find that, with a 400mm lens, a rifle-grip is the most effective means of support, allowing the most photographic opportunities. The photographs of the juvenile Semipalmated Plover (p. 63) and the juvenile Western Sandpiper (p. 95) were taken in this way. To reduce camera shake, use the marksman's technique of breathing out just before firing the shutter. With less approachable birds, a longer-focal-length lens is essential, and camera shake becomes more of a problem. The type of support is then one of personal preference, the usual choices being between monopod and tripod. Examples here of shorebirds photographed by stalking are the winter Bar-tailed Godwits (p. 149), taken with 600mm lens and ×1.4 converter using a monopod, and the winter Short-billed Dowitchers (Fig. 4, p. 28; and p. 138), taken with a 600mm lens on a tripod.

Finally, don't skimp on film. The problems of unexpected movements of the bird, combined with those of precise focusing and avoiding camera shake, are such that most shorebird photographers will be quite content with one satisfactory shot in four or five – and outstanding pictures come much less frequently than that!

THE SPECIES ACCOUNTS

Each species account follows a standard format, shown below.

Species *Scientific name*
Occurrence and migrant status in the N Atlantic area;
common names are given if these differ between the two
continents.
Identification   L = overall length from bill tip to end of
tail, and WS = wing-span, in centimetres (and inches). A
general statement of relative overall size, colouring,
proportionate bill and leg lengths, etc. Morphological
differences between sexes. Flight pattern. Usual feeding
method.

Juvenile
First-winter/adult winter
First-summer
Adult summer

{ Descriptions of plumage which
enable the different ages and
sexes to be distinguished *in the
field*. First-summer is not
described for species in which
most individuals of this age
acquire adult summer plumage.

Call   Brief description of most usual call or calls.
Status, habitat and distribution   As these apply in
N Atlantic area.
Racial variation   Morphological and plumage differences
between the races occurring in N Atlantic.
Similar species   Summary of the main distinguishing
features of similar species.
References   Further reading on identification, ageing,
sexing and racial differences (but not including the main
references acknowledged in the Introduction).

Table 3. Descriptions of shorebird size, bill length and leg length used in this book

Size	Very small	Small	Medium-sized	Large	Very large
Overall length	<15.9 cm	16–21.9 cm	22–32.9 cm	33–49.9 cm	>50 cm
Bill length	Very short	Short	Medium-length	Long	Very long
Bill/Overall length Ratio	<0.08	0.08–0.12	0.13–0.17	0.19–0.22	>0.22
Leg length	Short	Medium-length	Long	Very long	
Tarsus/ Overall length Ratio	<0.13	0.13–0.17	0.18–0.23	>0.23	

It is difficult to give a measurement that relates with any precision to the overall dimensions of a shorebird seen in the field. The figures that are quoted in the text enable the sizes of different species to be compared, but they are not in any sense absolute measurements. Overall size is indicated by the bird's length, from bill tip to end of tail, when placed on a flat surface. This is the usual measurement quoted in field guides, and is referred to here as the 'overall length'. The figures are taken from Hayman et al. (1986); it should be appreciated that they represent average sizes for the species concerned, and that individuals may vary in size from that indicated. The overall length is the basis of the size category used, as shown in Table 3.

The wing-spans enable comparisons to be made of the apparent size of birds in flight; where possible these measurements are from freshly dead birds, their wings spread using reasonable, not exceptional, force. It is found (Holden 1985) that this measurement is about three times the measurement of the 'wing length' (from the bend of the wing to the tip of the longest primary) using the flattened straightened wing technique (e.g. Prater et al. 1977). The average of this ratio for shorebirds as a group is about 3.1, and thus, for species where wing-span measurements are not available, the wing length from either Prater et al. (1977) or Hayman et al. (1986) is multiplied by 3.1 to give the wing-span. As Holden pointed out, this method yields wing-spans that are considerably less than those quoted by Cramp & Simmons (1983).

The categories of relative bill and leg lengths are obtained by expressing the bill or tarsus length as a ratio of the overall length of the bird, and these categories are also defined in Table 3. Some discretion has been used with the leg-length classifications, since the proportionate leg length should also include the length of the tibia (for which measurements are not available), not just that of the tarsus. For example, the Mountain Dotterel's tarsus length indicates 'long' legs, whereas they are better described as being of 'medium-length'; similarly, the Willet has 'long', not 'medium-length' legs.

Photo captions

The captions summarize the main points of interest of the photograph. For each photograph the location is given, since geographical location can be helpful in attempting to decide the race or population to which the individual may belong. Similarly, it is valuable to know the date on which the photograph was taken; consequently, so far as possible, the month is given, qualified by 'early' (1st to 10th day of the month), 'mid' (11th to 20th), or 'late' (on or after 21st).

For plumage terminology, it may be helpful to refer to the Frontispiece or to Fig.1 , p. 24.

Northern Pied Oystercatcher (Oystercatcher)
Haematopus ostralegus
A European and Asiatic partial migrant.

Identification L43 (17″); WS76 (30″). Large, with long, straight, laterally compressed orange or blackish-tipped orange bill and short pink legs. Head, neck, upperparts and wing-coverts (except greater coverts) black or brownish-black; greater coverts and underparts white. Sexes of similar size; adult male's slightly shorter, deeper bill may enable pairs seen together to be sexed. Bill pointed on individuals that feed by probing, chisel-tipped on shellfish feeders. In flight (p. 194), black above with broad white wing-bar, and white rump extending in V up back; black tail-band, narrower in juvenile and first-winter; feet do not reach end of tail. Feeds on shellfish, and also by probing to moderate depths.

Juvenile Head and neck dull sooty-black; no white half-collar on foreneck; upperparts and wing-coverts brownish-black, indistinctly scalloped with narrow paler fringes. Blackish-tipped, orange-yellow pointed bill; legs greyish-pink; iris brown, inconspicuous orbital ring.

First-winter Upperparts brownish-black; irregular white half-collar on foreneck; bare parts much as juvenile. Retains some juvenile wing-coverts, but best aged by combination of brownish upperparts and dull bare-part colours.

First-summer to third-winter As adult winter, but has broad white foreneck collar. Bare-part colours are transitional between first-winter and adult winter.

Adult winter Upperparts black; irregular white foreneck collar, narrower than that of immatures. Bill orange; legs pink; iris red; orbital ring orange-red.

Adult summer As adult winter, but loses white half-collar; bare parts brighter.

Call A strident, piping 'kleep', and 'kip, kip'.

Status, habitat and distribution Common in W Europe, not recorded in N America. The nominate race *H. o. ostralegus* generally breeds near the coast, from Iceland, Britain and Ireland, Norway and Sweden, south to France and locally around N Mediterranean. Winters from Britain and Ireland and Denmark, south to Africa; vagrant to Greenland and Spitsbergen.

Racial variation Other races seem unlikely to occur in W Europe.

Similar species Confusion possible only with American Oystercatcher, which has a proportionately longer, deeper, less orange bill, a yellow iris, has no white half-collar and (in flight) lacks white V up back.

Reference Dare & Mercer 1974.

Northern Pied Oystercatcher
juvenile Aged by brownish-black upperparts, lack of white foreneck collar, dark iris, bill with extensive black tip, and flesh-coloured legs. N Wales, mid-August. *RJC*

Northern Pied Oystercatcher
first-summer Aged by broad white foreneck collar, blackish bill tip (less extensive than on juvenile), and pinkish-flesh legs. The long tail extension beyond the primaries suggests that this bird is in wing moult. N Wales, mid-August. *RJC*

Northern Pied Oystercatcher
adult summer Aged by black upperparts, red iris, entirely orange bill and pink legs. Note less pointed bill tip than juvenile. N Wales, mid-August. *RJC*

43

American Oystercatcher *Haematopus palliatus*

A mainly sedentary American species.

Identification L42 (16.5"); WS76 (30"). Large, with long, straight, laterally-compressed blackish- or yellowish-tipped orange bill and medium-length pale pink legs. Head and neck black, upperparts and wing-coverts (except greater coverts) brownish-black; greater coverts and underparts white. Sexes of similar size; pairs seen together may perhaps be sexed by the male's slightly shorter bill. In flight, black above, with white wing-bar on secondaries (just extending to primaries in nominate race), and white uppertail-coverts; feet do not reach end of tail. Feeds on shellfish, and also by probing to moderate depths.

Juvenile Head and neck black, with off-white spots; upperparts brownish-black, scalloped with closely spotted buff fringes. Darkish-tipped brownish-pink pointed bill; legs grey; iris brown, inconspicuous orbital ring.

First-winter Much as juvenile, though bare-part coloration is brighter. Upperparts have buff fringes following post-juvenile moult, but the scalloped appearance is reduced by wear; retains some juvenile wing-coverts.

First-summer to third-winter Bare-part colours are transitional, as with Northern Pied Oystercatcher.

Adult winter/adult summer Head and neck black; upperparts brownish-black, mantle and scapulars fringed paler in winter, becoming more uniform with wear during summer. Bright orange, yellow-tipped bill; legs flesh, becoming pale pink in summer; iris yellow, orbital ring orange-red. Male has blacker upperparts and brighter bare parts.

Call A strident, piping 'kleep', and 'kip, kip'.

Status, habitat and distribution Uncommon along the coast in USA, vagrant in E Canada; unrecorded in Europe. The nominate race breeds from New England south to Florida and the Gulf Coast, and winters from Delaware south to C America.

Racial variation Other races seem unlikely to occur in eastern N America.

Similar species Northern Pied Oystercatcher has a proportionately less deep, shorter, and brighter orange bill, is black not brown on upperparts, and has a white half-collar on foreneck in winter plumages; in flight, white rump of Northern Pied Oystercatcher extends in a *V* up back. The all-black, near-sedentary American Black Oystercatcher *H. bachmani* has not occurred in eastern N America.

American Oystercatcher
adult Aged by yellow iris and yellow-tipped (not dark-tipped) bill. Unlike adult Northern Pied Oystercatcher, has brownish-black upperparts. Florida, mid-January. *RJC*

Black-winged/Black-necked Stilt *Himantopus himantopus*

Occurs in Europe ('Black-winged') and N America ('Black-necked').

Identification L36.5 (14.5″); WS69 (27″). Large, with medium-length, needle-fine, straight black bill and very long red legs. Elegant, long-necked and slender-bodied; white below, with variable amounts of black or grey on head and hindneck; black upperparts and wings. Male typically 10% larger than female. In flight (p. 195), has uniform black wings (but see below) with white uppertail-coverts, and white rump extending in *V* up back; greyish tail; legs and feet project well beyond tail, tail-tip reaching only to knee. Feeds by wading, picking from the water surface and sweeping bill from side to side.

Juvenile Cap and hindneck grey or black depending on race; upperparts and wing-coverts blackish-brown with buff fringes; underparts white; male has greenish sheen to wing-coverts. White tips to inner primaries and secondaries show in flight. Legs pinkish-grey; reddish base to lower mandible.

First-winter/first-summer As juvenile, but upperparts grey-black, initially paler with pale fringes; retains many juvenile wing-coverts. Legs red.

Adult winter/adult summer Black on cap and hindneck variable, depending upon race and sex. Mantle and scapulars black in male, very dark brown in female; wing-coverts black. Bill completely black; legs red, brighter in summer.

Call A noisy, resonant 'kek'.

Status, habitat and distribution Common in suitable wetland with shallow water. The nominate race (Black-winged Stilt) breeds from

France to N Africa, the majority moving south of the Mediterranean in winter. Vagrants occur north to Britain, Ireland and Sweden; not recorded in eastern N America. N American race *H. h. mexicanus* (Black-necked Stilt) breeds in coastal areas south from Delaware, wintering in Florida (uncommonly) and in Central and S America. Has occurred as far north as Newfoundland in spring.

Racial variation Differences involve head and neck patterns. *H. h. himantopus*: juvenile has greyish cap and hindneck which is retained through the first summer; adult winter/summer has varying amounts of black on cap and hindneck in both sexes, female having white fringes and streaks in black areas; neck greyish in winter. *H. h. mexicanus*: in all plumages has black crown, nape, ear-coverts and hindneck, with small white area above and slightly behind eye.

Similar species None.

Black-winged Stilt
juvenile Aged by brownish upperparts and wing-coverts, though is already acquiring some greyish first-winter feathers. Bulgaria, mid-August.
J. Lawton Roberts

Black-necked Stilt
juvenile Greenish gloss on wing-coverts indicates a male. California, mid-September. *RJC*

Black-winged Stilt
adult winter Aged
by dirty-greyish neck;
brownish mantle
indicates a female.
Gambia, mid-
January. *RJC*

Black-winged Stilt
adult summer Aged
by uniform black
upperparts (which
indicate a male;
female has brownish-
black mantle) and
wing-coverts.
S France, early July.
Richard T. Mills

Black-necked Stilt
adult summer Male.
Florida, late March.
Gordon Langsbury

Pied Avocet (Avocet) *Recurvirostra avosetta*
A mainly migratory Eurasian and African species.
Identification L43 (17"); WS67 (26.5"). Large, with long, upturned, slender black bill, long neck and long bluish-grey legs. Forehead, crown, hindneck, upper scapulars, greater coverts and outer primaries black; remainder white. Sexes of similar size, but female tends to have a shorter, more curved bill, which may enable pairs seen together to be sexed. In flight from above (p. 195), wings strikingly patterned black and white; rump and tail white; below, only primaries are black; legs and feet extend some way beyond tail. Feeds while wading (often swims), continuously scything bill from side to side, but will pick from surface of mud or water.
Juvenile Pattern as adult, but with brownish markings on white mantle, wing-coverts and tail, and pale fringes on sooty-brown tertials, which together give an overall 'dirty' appearance. Black areas duller and browner than in adults.
First-winter As juvenile, but mantle white; some juvenile wing-coverts are retained; upper scapulars fringed white.
Adult winter/adult summer Entirely black and white, except for brownish tertials. White oval area formed by lower scapulars and wing-coverts very pale grey in winter, bleaching to white in summer. Some individuals have legs tinged yellow.
Call 'Kluit'.
Status, habitat and distribution Fairly common on coasts or coastal wetlands with areas of alkaline or saline shallow water. Breeds locally from S Sweden to the Mediterranean. Winters on coasts of S England and southern North Sea, south to Mediterranean and N Africa. Not recorded in N America.
Racial variation No races recognized.
Similar species Sharply upturned bill and pied plumage distinguish Pied Avocet from all but American Avocet, which has no black on head but significantly more black on wings, both when standing and in flight.

Pied Avocet
juvenile Aged by brownish-tinged feathers on upperparts and 'scalloped' brownish-black wing-coverts. E England, late July. *RJC*

Pied Avocet
adult summer Aged by entirely black and white plumage, apart from brownish tertials; longish, gently upcurved bill suggests that this is a male. E England, early June. *RJC*

Pied Avocet
adult summer Aged as above; shortish, more strongly upcurved bill suggests a female. E England, late April. *RJC*

American Avocet *Recurvirostra americana*
Migratory N American species.
Identification L45 (17.5″); WS68 (27″). Large, with long, upturned, slender black bill, long neck and long bluish-grey legs. Black and white body with (depending on age and season) greyish or rust-brown head and neck. Upperparts and folded wings mainly black or brownish, with white mantle and white band extending across wing-coverts and lower scapulars. Underparts white. Male marginally larger, with longer, less curved bill than female. In flight from above, has outer wing black, inner wing white with black bar across greater coverts; body white, with black stripe on upper scapulars; rump and tail white; below, only primaries are black; legs and feet extend some way beyond tail. Generally feeds while wading (often swims), by scything bill from side to side, but may pick items from mud or surface of water.
Juvenile Head and neck cinnamon; white mantle and wing-coverts have brownish tips.
First-winter/adult winter Head and neck pale grey. First-winter retains some worn juvenile brown-tipped wing-coverts.
Adult summer Head and neck rusty-brown, brighter in male.
Call A far-carrying 'kleek'.
Status, habitat and distribution Fairly common, often in flocks, on fresh, saline and alkaline shallow waters. Breeds in west and central N America from Saskatchewan to S California and Texas. Along east coast, winters from N Carolina to Florida, the Gulf and further south. Not recorded in Europe.
Racial variation No races recognized.
Similar species Upturned bill and pied plumage eliminate all but Pied Avocet.

American Avocet
adult winter Slightly shorter, more strongly upcurved bill suggests a female. California, early January. *Arnoud B. van den Berg*

American Avocet
adult summer Longer, straighter bill suggests a male. USA, date unknown. *A. Cruickshank/ VIREO*

Northern Thick-knee (Stone-curlew) *Burhinus oedicnemus*
A Eurasian and N African partial migrant.
Identification L42 (16.5"); WS79 (31"). Large, predominantly pale brown, with large yellow eye, short black-tipped yellow bill and long yellow legs. Narrow whitish band across lesser coverts on folded wing. Generally looks hunched, large-headed and short-necked. Sexes of similar size. In flight, upperwing shows black primaries with white flashes, black primary coverts and secondaries, and two white bars across brown inner wing-coverts; underwing white, with fairly broad black trailing edge; feet do not project beyond tail. Feeds mainly at night, stalking heron-like before stabbing at prey on the ground or in low vegetation.
Juvenile Similar to adult, but distinguished by lack of dark border to buffy-white lesser-covert bar (latter is broader than on adult) and broader, whiter tips to greater coverts. Plain face, usually lacking obvious supercilium. Often retains tail-down for some weeks after fledging.
First-winter/adult winter/adult summer Similar plumages the year round. Males show darker, more contrasting lower dark border to white lesser-covert bar, and more contrasting head pattern.
Call A series of fluty whistles, 'cur-lee, cur-lee', with rising inflexion, given particularly at night during breeding season.
Status, habitat and distribution Uncommon on dry, open, frequently stony terrain, often inland. Breeds from E England south to Spain (*B. o. oedicnemus*) and the Mediterranean basin (nominate *oedicnemus* in Europe, *B. o. saharae* in N Africa). Northerly breeders migrate south to winter on both sides of the Mediterranean, and perhaps in Africa south of the Sahara; S European birds may be resident all year. Vagrant to Ireland, Scotland, Denmark and north to Sweden. Does not occur in N America.
Racial variation Nominate race is rather darker than the more sandy *saharae*, but they are doubtfully distinguishable in the field.
Similar species None in N Atlantic area.
Reference Green & Bowden 1986.

Northern Thick-knee
juvenile Only a trace of white above the eye. E England, August. *Rhys Green*

Northern Thick-knee
adults Aged by stronger facial pattern and more contrasty wing-covert pattern than juvenile. Male, left, has blacker borders to white wing-covert bar. E England, mid-May. *Gordon Langsbury*

Collared Pratincole *Glareola pratincola*

S European/Asiatic migrant species.

Identification L25 (10″); WS58 (23″). Medium-sized, with very short, broad, red-based dark bill and short dark legs. Elongated shape owing to long pointed wings and long tail, which reaches to or just beyond folded wings. Upperparts and wing-coverts uniform dull brown (adult), primaries and secondaries darker; throat and upper foreneck creamy, bordered with streaks (adult winter) or thin black line (adult summer); breast brownish, rest of underparts white. Sexes of similar size. In flight from above, shows some contrast between wing-coverts and darker primaries, has white trailing edge to secondaries, white rump and uppertail-coverts, and deeply forked tail; below (p. 195), white body contrasts with dark underwings, which have red-brown coverts and white trailing edge to secondaries; feet do not extend to base of forked tail. Feeds on insects in graceful, tern-like flight; gregarious.

Juvenile Mantle and scapulars are broadly tipped pale buff, with dark subterminal bands; wing-coverts less strongly patterned, with pale fringes; dark primaries have neat pale fringes. Breast diffusely streaked.

First-winter/adult winter As adult summer, but head is streaked and pale throat has streaked border. Post-juvenile moult is a complete one, including flight feathers; consequently first-winter is indistinguishable from adult winter.

Adult summer Unstreaked head; creamy throat neatly outlined in black. Lores black in male, browner in female, though the difference is difficult to see in the field.

Call A sharp nasal 'kik' or 'kittik' or combinations of these.

Status, habitat and distribution Uncommon, except in Spain; frequents open areas, usually near water, but is not necessarily coastal. A southern species, breeding in loose colonies around the Mediterranean. Winters in Africa, probably just south of Sahara. Vagrant north to Norway. Does not occur in N America.

Racial variation The nominate race occurs in the N Atlantic area: other races occur in Africa, but are unlikely to appear in Europe.

Similar species Black-winged Pratincole is darker, has entirely black underwing-coverts, and lacks white trailing edge to secondaries.

Collared Pratincole
juvenile Aged by
pale-fringed
upperparts and wing-
coverts, lacking
adult's throat pattern.
Probably of the
African race
fuelleborni. Malawi,
November.
D.A. Smith

Collared Pratincole
winter Aged by
plain upperparts and
lack of throat pattern.
From locality, race
fuelleborni. Kenya,
January.
J.F. Reynolds

Collared Pratincole
adult summer Aged
by throat pattern and
plain upperparts and
wing-coverts; extent
of black on lores
suggests that this
individual is a male.
Spain, mid-May.
R. Pop

Black-winged Pratincole *Glareola nordmanni*
A vagrant to W Europe.
Identification L24 (9.5"); WS61 (24"). Medium-sized, with short neck, very short broad bill with tiny area of red at base, and medium-length dark legs. In all plumages very similar to Collared Pratincole, though slightly darker. Male is marginally larger than female and has more black on lores in summer. The major distinguishing features from Collared Pratincole are as follows. Wings slightly longer and tail marginally shorter (with shallower fork), so wing-tips generally tend to fall beyond tail; this effect is less clear cut with juveniles. Legs slightly longer. In flight from above, is darker, with less contrast between wing-coverts and flight feathers than on Collared, and, particularly, lacks white trailing edge to secondaries; below, uniformly blackish underwings contrast with white body. As with Collared Pratincole, has complete post-juvenile moult, so first-winter and adult winter are indistinguishable.
Call Similar to that of Collared Pratincole, but apparently lower-pitched.
Status, habitat and distribution Rare. Breeds in open steppes in USSR north and east of Black Sea, to about 80°E. Winters in W and southern Africa. Vagrant to W Europe, north to Iceland and Scandinavia, mostly August–September. Has not occurred in N America.
Racial variation No races recognized.
Similar species Collared Pratincole.
Reference van den Berg 1985.

Black-winged Pratincole
juvenile Best separated from juvenile Collared Pratincole in flight. Netherlands, late August. *Arnoud B. van den Berg*

Black-winged Pratincole
winter Note extension of wing-tips beyond tail; aged by lack of throat pattern. Israel, October.
Paul Doherty

Little Ringed Plover *Charadrius dubius*

A European and Asiatic migrant species.

Identification L15 (6″); WS35 (14″). Small, short-necked, with short, black, rather pointed bill and medium-length pale legs. Prominent yellow orbital ring at all ages. Upperparts pale brownish-grey (adult) or buff (juvenile); white hindneck collar has a black lower border which continues as band across breast; remainder of underparts white. Sexes of similar size. In flight from above, is uniform (no wing-bar, though a thin line is formed by white tips of greater coverts), with white sides to dark-centred rump; underwing white; legs do not extend beyond tail. Feeds in manner typical of small plovers (p. 12).

Juvenile Head brown-buff, with small off-white area on forehead; dull yellow orbital ring. Upperparts and wing-coverts have darkish subterminal lines and pale fringes; breast-band brown, often broken at centre. Legs flesh.

First-winter/adult winter Head patterns much as juvenile, but darker across lores and ear-coverts. Upperparts uniform pale brownish-grey. First-winter retains some worn juvenile wing-coverts. Breast-band brownish-black. (Does not usually occur in Europe in these plumages.)

Adult summer Head pattern has black band from bill across lores and on to ear-coverts, enclosing eye, and also over fore-crown, bordered white behind, this white extending behind eye as short supercilium; forehead white. Male has lores and breast-band black, female black with brown admixed. Bright yellow orbital ring. Upperparts uniform pale brownish-grey. Tiny pinkish area at base of bill. Legs pinkish-flesh.

Call A disyllabic 'pee-oo', with downward inflexion.

Status, habitat and distribution Uncommon, breeding near fresh water in open gravelly areas, dried river beds, etc., from Sweden south throughout Europe and N Africa, but not in Iceland, Wales or Ireland. W European population thought to migrate through France, across Mediterranean to winter in Africa south of Sahara. Vagrant to Ireland. No eastern N American records.

Racial variation Only one race, *C. d. curonicus*, in N Atlantic area.

Similar species Slighter build, prominent yellow orbital ring, absence of obvious wing-bar in flight, and combination of all-black bill and (usually) flesh-pink legs are sufficient to eliminate other ringed-plovers.

Little Ringed Plover
juvenile Aged by generally buffish upperparts with pale markings and darkish fringes; a very young individual, still retaining tail-down.
E England, late July.
RJC

Little Ringed Plover
adult winter This individual already has much black on face and breast. Gambia, mid-January. *RJC*

Little Ringed Plover
adult summer Aged by strong black markings on head and breast-band, worn upperparts and wing-coverts; lack of brown admixed in black indicates a male. E England, early July. *RJC*

Little Ringed Plover
adult summer Brown in facial markings and breast-band indicates a female. S England, early June. *Gordon Langsbury*

Ringed Plover *Charadrius hiaticula*
European and Asiatic migrant; small population in NE Canada.
Identification L19 (7.5″); WS36.5 (14.5″). Small, short-necked, with very short, blunt-tipped bill and medium-length yellow-orange legs. Has restricted webbing between outer and middle toes only. Adult summer male sometimes has thin yellow-orange orbital ring. Brownish-grey upperparts, shade varying with race; white hind-collar has black lower border which continues as black or brown band around breast; remainder of underparts white. Sexes of similar size; some racial variation. In flight from above (p. 196), shows a white central wing-bar, white patches on sides of rump, and dark tail with white on sides and tip; underwing white; feet do not extend beyond tail. Feeds in manner typical of small plovers (p. 12).
Juvenile Upperparts and wing-coverts dull greyish-brown, with dark subterminal lines and pale fringes; ear-coverts and fairly broad breast-band dark brown, latter sometimes broken at centre. Bill black; legs dull yellow-orange.
First-winter/adult winter Uniform greyish-brown upperparts. Breast-band and ear-coverts dark brown, black from mid-winter. First-winter retains some worn juvenile wing-coverts (*C. h. tundrae* only until winter). Small yellow area at base of bill; legs orange.
Adult summer As winter, but head pattern has black from base of bill, around eye to ear-coverts, and over fore-crown. White supercilium behind eye only. Bill orange, with black tip. Male at height of breeding season often has thin yellow-orange orbital ring; ear-coverts and breast-band black; female has brown admixed in black head pattern.
Call Fluty 'too-i', with upward inflexion.
Status, habitat and distribution Common, breeding in stony coastal areas, and in north of range inland on tundra. Away from breeding areas, generally coastal. *C. h. hiaticula* breeds from NE Canada, Greenland and Iceland to W Europe, while *C. h. tundrae* breeds in N Scandinavia and USSR. Most northerly birds of both races (including those from Canada) winter in Africa; more southerly breeders winter in coastal areas south from Netherlands, Britain and Ireland. In spite of breeding in NE Canada, there are no records from east N America away from breeding grounds.
Racial variation Race *tundrae* is smaller and darker than *hiaticula*; the two may, with direct comparison, be separable.
Similar species Semipalmated Plover.

Ringed Plover
juvenile Aged by
poorly defined
brownish-black head
markings, incomplete
breast-band, and
pale-fringed
upperparts and wing-
coverts. England,
late August. *RJC*

Ringed Plover
winter Similar head
markings and breast-
band to juvenile, but
lacks latter's pale
feather fringes.
Gambia, mid-
January. *RJC*

Ringed Plover
adult summer Black
head pattern and
breast-band, and
black-tipped orange
bill; male has black
markings and narrow
yellow orbital ring.
E England, late April.
RJC
Insert Female, with
brown admixed in
black of head and
breast-band.
E England, late
June. *RJC*

Semipalmated Plover *Charadrius semipalmatus*

A migratory N American species; vagrant to W Europe.

Identification L18 (7″); WS37 (14.5″). Small, short-necked and round-headed, with very short, rather pointed bill and medium-length yellow-orange legs. Has a limited amount of webbing between all three front toes. Narrow yellow orbital ring in all plumages. Dull medium-brown upperparts; white hindneck collar has black lower border which continues as black or brown breast-band; remainder of underparts white. Sexes of similar size. In flight from above (p. 196), shows a white wing-bar, white patches at sides of rump, and dark tail outlined white on sides and tip; underwing white; legs do not extend beyond tail. Feeds in manner typical of small plovers (p. 12).

Juvenile Upperparts and wing-coverts dull medium-brown with dark subterminal lines and pale fringes; ear-coverts and breast-band dark brown. Bill black, with small yellow patch at base; legs dull yellow.

First-winter/adult winter Uniform upperparts. Breast-band and ear-coverts dark brown. First-winter retains some worn juvenile wing-coverts. Small yellow-orange area at base of bill; legs orange.

Adult summer As adult winter, but head pattern has black from base of bill, around eye to ear-coverts, and over fore-crown. White forehead; supercilium behind eye only, smaller and often lacking on male. Breast-band black in male, brownish in female. Bill orange with black tip.

Call A distinctive 'chee-wit', with rising inflexion.

Status, habitat and distribution Common, breeding on gravelly or sandy areas, both on the coast and inland on the tundra, from N Canada to Newfoundland and Nova Scotia. Winters from S Carolina to S America. Extremely rare vagrant to Europe during September–November.

Racial variation No races recognized.

Similar species Distinguished from very similar Ringed Plover by call, webbing between all three toes, marginally smaller size and slighter build, more rounded head and more attenuated bill; in all plumages shows a yellow orbital ring (generally absent in Ringed Plover) and narrower breast-band. Unlike Ringed Plover, adult male typically lacks white supercilium behind eye. Slightly more restricted wing-bar of adult Semipalmated is of doubtful field value.

References Chandler 1987a, b; Dukes 1980.

Semipalmated Plover
juvenile Aged by indistinct facial pattern, dull breast-band, and pale-fringed upperparts and wing-coverts; note narrow orbital ring. (See also p. 13.) California, early September.
RJC

Semipalmated Plover
first-winter Indistinct facial pattern; heavily worn wing-coverts and tertials suggest a first-winter, rather than adult winter. Florida, late January.
RJC

Semipalmated Plover
adult Though strictly in winter plumage, has the black facial pattern and breast band of a summer male, but lacks an orange-based bill. Note virtual absence of supercilium compared with Ringed Plover. Florida, mid-September.
RJC

Wilson's Plover *Charadrius wilsonia*

N American short-distance migrant.

Identification L18.5 (7.5″); WS36 (14″). Small, short-necked, rather square-headed, with short, heavy black bill and medium-length flesh-coloured legs. White forehead joins supercilium; white eye-ring is particularly obvious below eye, where it contrasts with dark ear-coverts. Uniform brownish-grey upperparts; white hindneck collar not quite continuous across nape. Breast-band is sometimes incomplete; remainder of underparts white. Sexes of similar size. In flight from above, has a white wing-bar, white patches at sides of darkish-centred rump, and dark tail is fringed white; underwing white; feet extend just beyond tail. Feeds in more leisurely manner than most small plovers, often using its strong bill to take small crabs.

Juvenile Upperparts and wing-coverts appear scalloped, having pale buff fringes; pale brown breast-band is sometimes incomplete. Legs dull flesh.

First-winter/adult winter Uniform upperparts; breast-band pale brown to medium-brown, sometimes broken at centre. First-winter retains at least some worn juvenile wing-coverts. Legs dull flesh.

Adult summer Male has black bar on fore-crown, black line from bill across lores to lower margin of ear-coverts, and black breast-band. Female as adult winter. Legs pinkish-flesh.

Call High-pitched, whistled 'whit'.

Status, habitat and distribution A fairly common, entirely coastal species, occurring on open beaches, muddy areas and saltmarsh. The nominate race breeds from N Jersey south to Florida and around the Gulf Coast, moving south to winter from S Florida south to Brazil. There are no European records.

Racial variation Only the nominate race occurs in the N Atlantic area.

Similar species Head pattern and, particularly, the heavy bill and flesh-coloured legs separate Wilson's Plover from other small N American ringed-plovers.

Wilson's Plover
first-winter Aged by incomplete brownish breast-band and by worn, pale-fringed wing-coverts which contrast with fairly fresh upperparts. Florida, mid-January. *RJC*

Wilson's Plover
adult winter Upperparts and wing-coverts are uniformly fresh; Florida, mid-September. *RJC*

Wilson's Plover
adult summer Black fore-crown, lores and breast-band indicate a male. Florida, mid-April. *Gordon Langsbury*

Killdeer *Charadrius vociferus*

A migratory N American species; vagrant to Europe.

Identification L25 (10"); WS48 (19"). Medium-sized, with short black bill, rounded head, longer neck than other ringed-plovers, and medium-length pale yellowish or pinkish legs. Long tail projects well beyond folded wings, giving an elongate appearance. Upperparts dull brown; white hindneck collar and, uniquely in N Atlantic area, two black breast-bands; remainder of underparts white. Orange-red orbital ring in all plumages. Sexes of similar size. In flight from above (p. 196), shows white wing-bar and longish rusty-orange, white-edged but dark-ended tail; underwing white; feet do not reach tip of tail. Feeds in typical plover manner, sometimes in flocks outside breeding season.

Juvenile Head pattern lacks black; underparts and wing-coverts indistinctly fringed buff. Often retains tail-down streamers for a week or so after fledging.

First-winter/adult winter Usually some black in facial pattern. Mantle, scapulars and replaced wing-coverts have rufous fringes. First-winter retains some juvenile wing-coverts, but these can be distinguished only until mid-winter.

Adult summer Upperparts uniform brown. Black line from bill below eye to ear-coverts, and black bar from eye over fore-crown. White of forehead extends as thin line below eye; short white supercilium behind eye. Crown and upper nape brown. Female usually has more brown than male on lores, ear-coverts and breast-bands, but sexes safely separable only in breeding pairs.

Call A plaintive, far-carrying 'kill-dee'.

Status, habitat and distribution Common in open lowland grassy areas inland and on the coast. Breeds throughout N America south from Ontario, Quebec and Newfoundland. Winters south from Massachusetts. Rare vagrant to W Europe, most frequently between November and March.

Racial variation No other races in N America.

Similar species Double breast-band and rather larger size safely separate Killdeer from all other N Atlantic ringed-plovers; downy young, however, has only one breast-band.

Killdeer

Winter adults These two individuals, both in fresh plumage, were photographed together and are presumably a pair. The male (above) shows slightly more black on head and breast than the female (below), but the differences are small. In summer the black on the head is more extensive. Florida, mid-September. *RJC*

→ **Piping Plover** *Charadrius melodus*
A migratory N American species.
Identification L18.5 (7.5"); WS36 (14"). Small, with round head, very short blunt bill and short yellow-orange legs. Upperparts uniform pale sandy-brown or sandy-grey, with white hindneck collar and complete or incomplete breast-band. Underparts white except for breast-band. Sexes of similar size. In flight above (p. 196), has a prominent white wing-bar, while white uppertail-coverts form diagnostic band across full width of dark-ended tail; underwing white; feet do not extend beyond tail. Feeds in similar manner to other ringed-plovers (p.12).
Juvenile Head pattern rather plain, coloured as upperparts, with white forehead and supercilium and dark eye. Indistinctly scaly above, with somewhat paler fringes to upperparts and wing-coverts. Greyish breast-band incomplete. Bill black.
First-winter/adult winter Uniformly pale above; greyish breast-band sometimes broken; otherwise much as juvenile. First-winter retains some worn juvenile wing-coverts.
Adult summer As winter, but acquires black fore-crown bar and black breast-band, which is sometimes incomplete, especially in female. Bill orange-yellow with black tip; legs orange-yellow.
Call A plaintive 'peep'.
Status, habitat and distribution Uncommon, decreasing. Breeds on sandy shorelines, both coastally and by inland lakes in the prairies, around the eastern Great Lakes, and coastally from Quebec and Newfoundland south to Virginia. Winters from S Carolina to Florida, and on the Gulf Coast. Unrecorded in Europe.
Racial variation No races recognized.
Similar species Juvenile might be confused with juvenile Semipalmated Plover, but latter is marginally smaller, is darker with a more conspicuous breast-band, is more obviously scaly above, and has a more tapered bill. Snowy Plover is smaller, and does not have yellow legs. In flight, white uppertail-coverts are diagnostic of Piping Plover.

Piping Plover
winter The heavily worn wing-coverts and tertials suggest first-winter. Florida, mid-January. *RJC*

Piping Plover
adult summer
Completely black forehead bar and breast-band indicate a male. USA, early May. *G. LeBaron/ VIREO*

Kentish/Snowy Plover *Charadrius alexandrinus*
Migratory, with a widespread distribution; 'Snowy' in N America, 'Kentish' in Europe.
Identification L16.5 (6.5″); WS34 (13″). Small, round-headed, short-necked, with short, slender black bill and medium-length pale flesh (juvenile Snowy), greyish or blackish legs. Upperparts medium-grey (Kentish), paler in Snowy, with white hindneck collar; black or brown side-neck patches form a vestigial breast-band. Sexes of similar size. In flight from above (p. 70), shows a white wing-bar and extensive white on sides of tail; entirely white below; feet do not extend beyond tail. Feeds in manner typical of small plovers (p. 12).
Juvenile Head brown-grey, with white forehead running into white supercilium. Mantle, scapulars and tertials have black subterminal

lines and buff fringes; wing-coverts fringed buff. Breast-side patches relatively inconspicuous.

First-winter/adult winter As juvenile, but upperparts uniform, unscalloped; breast-side patches mid-brown. First-winter retains some juvenile buff-fringed wing-coverts. Legs often greyish.

Adult summer Male has black line of variable extent across lores through eye, extending as line or patch on to ear-coverts; black fore-crown bar; white forehead runs into white supercilium; black breast-side patches. Female has head pattern and breast-side patches brown where male is black, and is only marginally more contrasty than in juvenile or winter plumage. Legs usually blackish.

Call Kentish: a sharp, but quiet 'wit' and a harsher 'prrr'; Snowy: a quiet 'ku-wee', and a low 'knut'.

Status, habitat and distribution Fairly common in suitable habitat, breeding coastally on sandy beaches and by saline pools. Nominate *C. a. alexandrinus* (Kentish) breeds in Europe from extreme S Sweden and Denmark south to Mediterranean, but not in Britain or Ireland. Regular, but in small numbers, in E England on migration; vagrant to Ireland. Winters around Mediterranean and in Africa. *C. a. nivosus* (Snowy) breeds in N America in southern Great Plains and on the Gulf Coast, but is only occasional on east coast, where it occurs as a vagrant north to Ontario.

Racial variation Race *nivosus* is paler above than nominate *alexandrinus*, and has slightly shorter legs, which are pale flesh in juvenile. In breeding plumage, male *alexandrinus* usually has rusty-red crown (dull brown in *nivosus*), and has complete (or almost complete) black line between bill and eye which is often lacking in *nivosus*.

Similar species Piping Plover.

Snowy Plover
first-winter Aged by uniformly grey first-winter scapulars and panel of median coverts, which contrast with retained juvenile mantle and wing-coverts. California, October/November. *Eric & David Hosking*

Kentish Plover
adult winter
Uniformly fresh upperparts and wing-coverts; dark breast-side patches and black appearing on forehead suggest a male. Israel, early November. *Arnoud B. van den Berg*

Kentish Plover
adult summer
Poorly developed head pattern and brown breast-side patches indicate a female. Netherlands, early May. *R. Pop*

Kentish Plover
adult summer Black in head pattern and on breast-side patches indicates a male. Netherlands, early May. *R. Pop*
Insert Snowy Plover, *male*. This race lacks black between bill and eye. USA, date not known.
A Cruickshank/ VIREO

Mountain Dotterel (Dotterel) *Charadrius morinellus*

A migrant European and Asiatic species; also breeds in Alaska.

Identification L21 (8.5″); WS46 (18″). Small, with rounded head, prominent dark eye and short black bill, medium-length neck and medium-length yellowish legs. Rather scaly brown upperparts, dark crown, and broad pale supercilia meeting in *V* at hindneck. Underparts yellowish-buff with pale crescentic breast-band; dark belly in summer adult. Sexes of similar size. In flight from above, is uniformly brown; below, pale, with dark belly of summer adult clearly visible; feet do not extend beyond tail. Feeds by picking from ground or vegetation, in rather less of a 'stop-start' manner than other plovers.

Juvenile Crown dark, with buff supercilium. Mantle and scapulars dark brown with strongly contrasting fairly broad whitish fringes; wing-coverts similar, but less contrasty. Indistinct pale breast-band; underparts buff with strongly mottled foreneck; lower belly and undertail-coverts white.

First-winter/adult winter Mantle, scapulars and tertials more uniform than juvenile, with grey-brown centres and orange-buff fringes giving paler overall appearance. First-winter retains some juvenile wing-coverts and tertials, which are more contrasty than remainder of upperparts. (Does not usually occur in Europe in these plumages.)

Adult summer Crown dark, contrasting with white supercilium; throat white, neck and upper breast greyish; white breast-band has dark outline. Lower belly dark chestnut-brown. Sexes are basically similar, but female is generally brighter and more contrasty than male, which has white flecking on crown and largely white forehead.

Call A quiet trill, given particularly on take-off.

Status, habitat and distribution Uncommon, breeding on arctic tundra in Scotland, Scandinavia, Finland, N USSR and Asia; a scarce breeder in Alaska. Often occurs in small flocks ('trips') on migration, when it uses traditional 'staging posts' in open areas with very short, sparse vegetation. Whole population winters in semi-desert in N Africa and the Middle East. Scarce or vagrant in Europe outside its breeding range; no east N American records.

Racial variation No races recognized.

Similar species Could be confused with any of the three slightly larger golden plover species, but Mountain Dotterel's prominent supercilium, whitish breast-band and yellowish legs should make separation straightforward.

Mountain Dotterel
juvenile Aged by dark-centred, pale-fringed upperpart feathers; see also Fig. 1 (p. 24). SW England, early September. *RJC*

Mountain Dotterel
adult summer Bright, contrasty plumage suggests a female. S England, early May. *Gordon Langsbury*

Mountain Dotterel
adult summer Limited extent of dark feathers on crown and belly may indicate male and/or commencement of body moult to adult winter. SW England, late August. *RJC*

American Golden Plover *Pluvialis dominica*

A strongly migratory N American species, vagrant to Europe.

Identification L26 (10.5"); WS54 (21"). Medium-sized, round-headed, with a prominent dark eye, short black bill and medium-length black legs. Underparts largely black in adult summer plumage. Distinguished with difficulty from the other two golden plovers, in comparison with which it is intermediate in size. Some individuals are indistinguishable from Pacific Golden Plover. Folded wings usually extend noticeably beyond tail; typically, four primary tips extend beyond tertials; sexes of similar size. In flight, is long-winged, plain and uniform above; below, underwing (including axillaries) is buff-grey, body white (with darker breast) on non-breeding birds, the black of underbody on breeding birds not extending on to wing; feet reach just beyond tail. Feeds in typical plover manner, often in flocks in winter.

Juvenile Head and neck greyish, white supercilium; upperparts, especially scapulars, greater coverts and tertials, spotted or spangled dull gold, remainder spangled white. Pale brown barring on belly.

First-winter/adult winter As juvenile, but with limited spangling on upperparts; foreneck and breast grey; belly white in adults. First-winter birds retain some barring on underparts, particularly on flanks. (Does not usually occur in N Atlantic area in these plumages.)

First-summer Rarely attains full black underparts.

Adult summer Upperparts strongly spangled gold and white; a continuous white area, composed of forehead, supercilium, and extension of latter broadening on sides of neck (but not extending on to flanks), separates the upperparts from black underparts, which extend from face and foreneck over whole of breast, flanks and belly to include the undertail-coverts. Female has more white mixed with black on underparts than male, but both sexes are variable.

Call Disyllabic, fairly high-pitched 'too-ee' or plaintive 'pe-weee', similar to calls of Pacific Golden Plover.

Status, habitat and distribution A fairly common inland species, breeding in arctic and sub-arctic tundra from NW Alaska east to Baffin Island. Migrates south through interior N America or via Hudson Bay to reach coast around New England, then over Atlantic to S America. Winters in grassland and wetlands in N Argentina and Uruguay, returning north via Mississippi and Missouri valleys; thus uncommon away from breeding areas. Vagrant to Europe, occurring most frequently during September and October.

Racial variation No races recognized.

American Golden Plover
juvenile Best aged by barred belly and flanks; note strong supercilium, wing-tips extending beyond tail, and generally greyish plumage. SW England, mid-October. *Gordon Langsbury*

American Golden Plover
winter Texas, early March. *R. Pop*

American Golden Plover
adult summer Completely black belly suggests a male; note that there is no white on flanks. Alaska, June. *R. van Meurs*

Similar species Mountain Dotterel. Distinguished from Pacific Golden Plover in juvenile plumage by greyer, duller, much less yellow appearance, and more barred belly; in breeding plumage by absence of white on flanks and undertail-coverts. From European Golden Plover by smaller size, proportionately longer legs, greater primary extension beyond tail, and buff-grey (not white) underwing-coverts and axillaries. See also Table 4. From Grey/Black-bellied Plover by smaller size, less bulky head and bill, less grey appearance in all plumages, and different flight pattern lacking black axillaries.

References Connors 1983; Pym 1982.

Table 4. Main distinguishing features of the golden plovers; note that the primary projection is that beyond the tertials.

Species	Build and Flight Pattern
American Golden Plover (p. 74)	Length 26 cm; fairly bulky; longish legs; folded wings extend beyond tail; long primary projection. No wing-bar; underwing-coverts and axillaries buff-grey. In flight, feet reach just beyond tail.
Pacific Golden Plover (p. 78)	Length 25 cm; relatively slender; fairly long legs; folded wings extend just beyond tail; short primary projection. No wing-bar; underwing-coverts and axillaries buff-grey. In flight, feet just reach end of tail.
European Golden Plover (p. 80)	Length 27.5 cm; bulky; shortish legs; folded wings just reach tail; shortish primary projection. Variable white wing-bar; underwing-coverts and axillaries white. In flight, feet do not reach end of tail.

Juvenile/Winter	*Adult Summer*

Juvenile/Winter	Adult Summer
Obvious white supercilium; head and neck greyish-brown; upperparts darkish, spangled yellow; underparts barred. *Winter*: duller version of juvenile, with greyish breast and white belly.	Brightly spangled above; white forehead, narrow white supercilium continuing to broad white area on side of neck. No white on flanks or undertail-coverts; face and rest of underparts black.
Yellowish supercilium; head and neck strongly tinged yellow; upperparts brightly spangled yellow; streaked yellowish breast, white belly, flanks indistinctly barred. *Winter*: much as juvenile, but breast and belly uniformly greyish.	Less brightly spangled above; white forehead and broad white supercilium continue as line down side of neck, across flanks, to largely white undertail-coverts; face and remainder of underparts black.
Indistinct supercilium; head and neck dull yellow-brown; upperparts spangled gold; breast spotted, belly barred. *Winter*: much as juvenile, but belly white, unbarred.	Less brightly spangled above; white forehead and supercilium continue as line down side of neck, across flanks, to white or largely white undertail-coverts; face and foreneck black or brown depending on race; rest of underparts black.

Pacific Golden Plover *Pluvialis fulva*
Vagrant to N Atlantic area.
Identification L25 (10″); WS49 (19″). Medium-sized, marginally smaller and somewhat brighter, but otherwise very similar in all plumages to American Golden Plover, from which a few individuals may prove indistinguishable. Folded wings extend only marginally beyond tail; only two/three primary tips extend beyond relatively long tertials. Plumages vary seasonally. Sexes of similar size. Feeding and flight pattern (p. 196) much as in American Golden Plover.
Juvenile Yellowish supercilium; head and neck strongly washed yellow, upperparts extensively spangled gold. Limited barring on sides of belly.
First-winter/adult winter Duller than juvenile, with less yellow, especially on foreneck, and less obvious spangling. First-winter birds retain some barring on belly; adults have a more uniformly pale greyish-brown belly. (Does not normally occur in N Atlantic area in these plumages.)
Adult summer As American Golden Plover, but supercilium broader, and white area separating upperparts from black underparts extends continuously from side of neck, along flanks to undertail-coverts, which are mainly white. Females typically have more white speckling on black underparts than males.
Call As those of American Golden Plover.
Status, habitat and distribution Breeds in arctic tundra in Asia, but in N America only in W Alaska. Winters in S Asia, the Pacific islands and Australasia. A very rare vagrant throughout the N Atlantic area.
Racial variation No races recognized, but forms intermediate between Pacific and European Golden Plovers occur. These are smaller than European Golden and have many of the characteristics of Pacific Golden, but with white axillaries.
Similar species American Golden Plover; see also Table 4, p. 76–7.
Reference Vinicombe 1988.

Pacific Golden Plover
juvenile In rather worn plumage, having lost yellow tints on neck and upperparts typical of fresh juvenile; aged by lightly barred flanks. Queensland, December. *T. & P. Gardener/Frank Lane*

Pacific Golden Plover
first-winter/summer Aged by combination of juvenile and winter tertials, both of which are worn. Japan, date not known. *C. Speegle/VIREO*

Pacific Golden Plover
adult summer Moulting into adult winter; note length of tertials. Australia, late August. *Brian Chudleigh*

79

European Golden Plover *Pluvialis apricaria*

Migratory, with a largely European distribution. Vagrant to N America. **Identification** L27.5 (11"); WS58 (23"). Medium-sized, round-headed, with short black bill and medium-length greyish legs. Slightly larger and rather more bulky than the other two golden plovers, lacking their stronger supercilium. Extent of black on underparts in summer depends on race, but is similar to that of Pacific Golden Plover. Folded primaries extend to, or only just beyond, tail; typically, shows three primary tips beyond tertials. Sexes of similar size. In flight from above (p. 196), shows a variable narrow white wing-bar formed by tips of greater coverts, broadening on to primaries; below, underwing-coverts and axillaries are white (secondaries and primaries greyish); feet do not extend beyond tail. Feeds in typical plover manner, often in flocks outside breeding season.

Juvenile The whole of the upperparts are brown, spangled gold, with some white spotting intermixed, particularly on the mantle. Scapulars and tertials have a broad dark shaft-streak reaching feather tip. Breast closely spotted, with brown barring on paler belly.

First-winter/adult winter Upperparts much as juvenile, though less bright; breast streaked, rather than spotted. Scapulars and tertials have thin or absent shaft-streak at tip. First-winter retains some juvenile wing-coverts and perhaps some barring on flanks; adults have white belly and lower flanks. Difficult to age in the field in the absence of flank barring.

Adult summer Bright gold and (to a lesser extent) white spangling on mantle and scapulars; breast and belly black; face, throat and foreneck black or brown, depending on race. Black or brown underparts have white border, the pattern being as that of Pacific Golden Plover. With breeding pairs, face pattern and underparts of female are generally seen to be browner, with scattered white feathers on belly.

Call A clear, yodelled 'loo-ee'.

Status, habitat and distribution A fairly common species, breeding on arctic and sub-arctic tundra in Iceland, northern Scandinavia, Finland and USSR (*P. a. altifrons*), and in Britain, Ireland and S Scandinavia (*P. a. apricaria*). Winters on grassland, often inland, in Britain and Ireland, Netherlands, and south to N Africa. Regular during migration in S Greenland; very rare vagrant to E Canada.

Racial variation The two races differ only in breeding plumage; individuals vary, but typical *altifrons* has prominent white supercilium and black face and foreneck, while *apricaria* is duller, with a less obvious supercilium and brown face and foreneck.

Similar species See American Golden Plover; also Table 4, p. 76–7.

European Golden Plover
juvenile Moulting into first-winter, but still retains light barring on flanks. (See also p. 14.) N Wales, late October. *RJC*

European Golden Plover
adult summer Brownish face and restricted black on belly suggest a female; note that wing-tips extend only just beyond tail. Iceland, early August. *R. Pop*

European Golden Plover
adult summer Extensive black on face and underparts suggests male of race *altifrons*. Norway, June. *Roger Tidman*

European Golden Plover
adult Moulting from summer to adult winter. SW England, early September. *RJC*

Grey/Black-bellied Plover *Pluvialis squatarola*

Widespread migrant; 'Black-bellied' in N America and 'Grey' in Europe.

Identification L28.5 (11.5″); WS59 (23″). Medium-sized and round-headed, with a prominent dark eye, short, slightly bulbous black bill and medium-length dark grey legs. Larger and more bulky than the superficially similar golden plovers, it is basically grey in all plumages, and, as with the golden plovers, adult summer has black underparts. The extent of black most resembles that of American Golden Plover, but the undertail-coverts are white. The only *Pluvialis* species with a hind toe. Sexes of similar size. In flight from above (p. 197), has outer wing blackish, with broad white wing-bar, inner wing uniformly grey; rump white, tail barred grey; below, whitish, but shows striking diagnostic black axillaries, which in adult summer are contiguous with the black underparts; feet just reach tip of tail. Feeds in typical, deliberate, plover manner.

Juvenile Darkish grey-brown crown, white supercilium. Mantle, scapulars and tertials dark grey-brown, with extensive very pale yellowish or buff spotting on feather edges, giving whitish-spangled appearance at a distance; wing-coverts similar, but paler and duller; foreneck and breast streaked.

First-winter/adult winter Head pattern less contrasty than juvenile; upperparts mid-grey, notched and fringed whitish. Neck and upper breast mottled or streaked grey, remainder of underparts white. First-winter birds usually retain a variable number of darker, worn juvenile feathers on upperparts, wing-coverts and tertials.

First-summer As adult winter, but gains a few black feathers on underparts.

Adult summer Crown greyish, nape and sides of neck white; mantle and scapulars black, spangled bright white; face, foreneck, breast and belly black; undertail-coverts white. Underparts of male black, with a few white-fringed feathers; those of female brownish-black, with many whitish feathers.

Call Plaintive 'pee-oo-eee', with downward inflexion on middle syllable.

Status, habitat and distribution A fairly common species, with a nearly circumpolar arctic breeding distribution (though not Greenland or N Scandinavia), breeding in tundra. Winters coastally on mudflats and beaches, from Netherlands, Britain and Ireland in Europe as far south as S Africa, in N America from New Jersey south to S Brazil. On both sides of the Atlantic females winter further south than males. Vagrant to Greenland, Iceland and Spitsbergen.

Racial variation No races recognized, but N American juveniles often have larger spots on upperparts than those in Europe.

Similar species Separated from the golden plovers by larger size, heavier bill and greyer appearance in all plumages, and, particularly, by flight pattern with white rump and diagnostic black axillaries.

Grey/Black-bellied Plover
juvenile Aged by contrasty, chequered upperparts and edge-spotted tertials. New Jersey, late September. *RJC*

Grey/Black-bellied Plover
first-winter Aged by one or two retained blackish juvenile upper scapulars. Florida, mid-January. *RJC*

Grey/Black-bellied Plover
adult winter Aged by uniformly dull upperparts, wing-coverts and tertials. New Jersey, late September. *RJC*

Grey/Black-bellied Plover
adult summer Uniform black belly suggests a male. Alaska, June. *R. van Meurs*

Northern Lapwing *Vanellus vanellus*

A migrant or partial migrant of Eurasia; vagrant to N America.

Identification L29 (11.5″); WS66 (26″). Medium-sized, with distinctive wispy crest, short black bill and medium-length pinkish or red legs. Overall appearance black and white, but upperparts have dark green metallic sheen; crown and crest black, sides of head and nape generally white; broad black neck/breast-band, which extends to bill in adult summer plumage; underparts white, but with rusty undertail-coverts. In flight (p. 197), broad rounded wings and 'flappy' flight, alternatively flashing black and white; from above, appears black, with pale tips to outer primaries, white uppertail and narrow white tail-tip (moulting summer adults often show white patches on wings); below, black primaries and secondaries contrast with broad white underwing-coverts and body; feet do not extend beyond tail. Width of outer wing depends on age and sex, adult male having particularly noticeable 'bulging' primaries. Feeds in typical plover manner.

Juvenile Short crest; obscure black markings on face. Dull metallic green upperparts, with narrow pale buff fringes composed of small spots. Throat white; breast-band feathers fringed white. Legs dull pink.

First-winter/adult winter As juvenile, but upperparts have brighter metallic green sheen, feathers more broadly tipped (not fringed) rich buff, these tips gradually wearing away. Fairly short crest. First-winter birds may retain a few juvenile pale-buff-fringed upperpart feathers and wing-coverts, but the fringes wear quickly.

Adult summer Buff fringes on upperparts wear off by early summer. Black of breast-band extends upwards, so that, on male, forehead, lores, chin and throat also become black. Female generally retains some white feathers on foreneck. Crest is longer on male.

Call A plaintive 'pee-wit', with rising inflexion.

Status, habitat and distribution A common, generally inland species, breeding in grassland and grassy wetlands throughout Europe (except N Scandinavia), south to France and, locally, central regions of Spain; rare breeder in Iceland and Faeroes. Extensive westerly movements of adults from E and C Europe to east North Sea area, Britain and Ireland commence in late May; westerly and southerly movements also occur in winter during hard weather. Winters from Britain and Ireland south to the Mediterranean shores of N Africa. Vagrant to Spitsbergen and eastern N America.

Racial variation No races recognized.

Similar species Wispy crest and dark green upperparts are diagnostic.

Northern Lapwing
juvenile Aged by narrow, pale-buff-spotted fringes of upperparts and wing-coverts. E England, early August. *RJC*

Northern Lapwing
adult winter Aged by broad rusty-buff tips to upperparts and wing-coverts. E England, mid-August. *RJC*

Northern Lapwing
adult summer Buff feather tips of winter plumage have worn off; long crest and all-black chin and breast suggest a male. E England, early July. *RJC*

Red Knot (Knot) *Calidris canutus*

A migrant species that occurs on both sides of the N Atlantic.

Identification L24 (9.5″); WS51 (20″). Medium-sized, shortish-necked, with medium-length dark grey or black bill and medium-length brownish-yellow legs. Plumages vary seasonally. Sexes of similar size. In flight from above (p. 197), fairly uniform apart from narrow white wing-bar and pale grey rump; feet do not project beyond tail. Feeds by methodical picking or probing to shallow depth.

Juvenile Prominent whitish supercilium. Upperparts brownish-grey; mantle, scapulars, wing-coverts and, to a lesser extent, tertials have thin dark submarginal lines and narrow whitish fringes, giving neatly scalloped appearance. Underparts, especially breast, lightly spotted and barred over pale salmon-pink wash. Bill grey or dark grey with black tip.

First-winter/adult winter Uniform grey upperparts, neatly fringed white when fresh. First-winter may retain some juvenile wing-coverts. Bill usually black.

Adult summer Mantle and scapulars dark brownish-black with large rusty spots and whitish fringes. Supercilium, face, foreneck, breast and most of belly brick-red. Females generally greyer above, and with scattered whitish feathers on underparts. Bill black.

Call A subdued 'knut'.

Status, habitat and distribution Locally common, breeding on drier upland tundra: *C. c. islandica* in N Greenland and the Canadian high-arctic islands; *C. c. rufa* in Canadian Arctic from Victoria Island to N Hudson Bay; *C. c. rogersi* in N Alaska and locally in high-arctic E

USSR; and *C. c. canutus* in C Siberia. Race *islandica* winters in W Europe, mainly from Ireland, Britain and Netherlands south to France and Portugal; *rufa* from Massachusetts south to S America, especially Argentina; *rogersi* in Australasia; and *canutus* in W and S Africa. In winter occurs almost exclusively on extensive coastal mudflats, often in very large flocks.

Racial variation Doubtfully separable in the field, in adult summer plumage only; *canutus* is darkest above and below, with limited white on undertail-coverts; *rufa* is paler above, paler red below, with more extensive white on undertail-coverts; *islandica* and *rogersi* are more or less intermediate.

Similar species Plumage of Red Knot at all ages is remarkably similar to that of Curlew Sandpiper, but former is obviously larger and more bulky, with shorter straight bill.

Red Knot
juvenile Aged by dark submarginal lines and pale fringes on upper parts; this individual has acquired a few plain grey first-winter scapulars.
NW England, September. *J.F. Reynolds*

Red Knot
adult winter Aged by fresh uniform grey upperparts and wing-coverts; race *rufa*.
Florida, mid-September. *RJC*

Red Knot
adult summer Fresh plumage; from location, identified as race *rufa*. Florida, late April. *Gordon Langsbury*

Red Knot
adult summer Commencing moult to winter plumage; race *islandica*. Ireland, early August. *Richard T. Mills*

Red Knot
adult In advanced moult to winter plumage; race *rufa*. Florida, mid-September. *RJC*

Sanderling *Calidris alba*

A long-distance migrant occurring on both sides of N Atlantic.

Identification L20 (8"); WS39 (15.5"). Small, with short, straight, heavyish black bill and short black legs. Only *Calidris* without a hind toe. Plumages vary seasonally. Sexes of similar size. In flight from above (p. 198), has a prominent white wing-bar (emphasized by darker outer wing), with rump and uppertail-coverts grey-centred with white sides; feet do not reach tail. Feeds generally on sandy beaches, running vigorously at the water's edge, pausing briefly to pick or probe.

Juvenile Darkish crown; mantle and scapulars chequered black and white, with marginal spots on black feathers; wing-coverts are variable with dark subterminal marks, or are plainer with pale fringes. White beneath.

First-winter/first-summer/adult winter Uniform pale grey above; first-winter birds in N Atlantic area usually retain their worn juvenile wing-coverts. Dark fore-wing may show at bend of folded wing; adults have larger scapulars which often obscure both dark fore-wing area and relatively unworn coverts. First-summer birds do not attain adult summer plumage.

Adult summer Whole of head, neck and upper breast rufous, spotted black; mantle and scapulars black with extensive whitish fringes when fresh, becoming more rufous with wear; coverts grey. Underparts white. Male more rufous on upperparts and upper breast than female, but sexes safely separable only in breeding pairs.

Call A staccato 'kip' or 'quick'.

Status, habitat and distribution A common species, widespread outside the breeding season. Breeds in the high Arctic on stony, well-drained tundra in Alaska, Canada south to Southampton Island, in N Greenland and locally in Asia. Winters from Britain, Ireland and Denmark south to S Africa, and from Massachusetts south to southern S America, typically on wide sandy beaches.

Racial variation No races recognized.

Similar species Single Sanderlings can suggest a stint or peep, the similarity in adult summer plumage to Rufous-necked Stint being particularly striking; see latter species. Greater size of Sanderling (slightly larger than Dunlin and Ringed or Semipalmated Plovers) rules out this confusion, as does absence of hind toe.

Sanderling
juvenile Aged by strongly chequered upperparts. Florida, late September. *RJC*

Sanderling
first-winter Aged by combination of uniform grey upperparts and worn juvenile tertials. Florida, mid-January. *RJC*

Sanderling
adult summer Note absence of hind toe, which eliminates Rufous-necked Stint. USA, date not known. *A. Morris/ VIREO*

91

Semipalmated Sandpiper *Calidris pusilla*

A migrant N American species; vagrant to Europe.

Identification L14 (5.5"); WS30 (12"). Very small, with a medium-length, straight, blunt-tipped black bill and medium-length black legs. A rather dull, short-billed stint. Partial webbing between toes. Short primary projection beyond tertials. Sexes of similar size, females having marginally longer bills. In flight from above, has a narrow white wing-bar and white sides to dark-centred rump; feet do not reach tail-tip. Feeds by picking from surface, sometimes wading.

Juvenile Whitish supercilium, accentuated by dark crown, loral line and ear-coverts; crown uniformly dark and rather coarsely streaked. Upperparts have dark grey-brown feather centres, with buff or off-white fringes and little or no mantle or scapular V; rear lower scapulars have dark anchor-shaped subterminal mark (Fig. 7, p. 96). Breast sides streaked dark, with buffish wash across upper breast.

First-winter/adult winter Upperparts and wing-coverts uniformly brownish-grey; underparts white, with diffuse streaking on sides of breast only. First-winter retains juvenile wing-coverts, which are more worn, browner, and more broadly fringed than in adult winter. (Does not usually occur in N America in these plumages.)

Adult summer Crown coarsely streaked. Rather dull upperpart feathers have dark centres and grey or yellowish-buff fringes. Breast and upper flanks strongly streaked.

Call Short, coarse 'chrup' or 'turp'.

Status, habitat and distribution Common, breeding in sub-arctic zone on northern edge of boreal forest, from Alaska to Baffin Island and Labrador. On passage and in winter generally uses coastal estuarine habitats, following a route from SE Canada either down coastal E USA or by direct flight to E Caribbean. E Canadian birds return northwards along east coast. Winters in coastal S America. Vagrant to W Europe.

Racial variation No races recognized, but E Canadian birds have on average slightly longer bills.

Similar species In N America long-billed individuals are most likely to be confused with Western Sandpiper, the only other *Calidris* species with partially webbed toes. Typically, Western Sandpiper has a longer, more decurved bill; juvenile has bright chestnut upper scapulars, and adult summer has much chestnut on upperparts and diagnostic small chevrons on breast and upper flanks. See also Table 5, p. 100–101.

References Jonsson & Grant 1984; Veit & Jonsson 1984; Wallace 1980c.

**Semipalmated
Sandpiper**
juvenile Aged by
neat, pale-fringed
upperparts and
scapulars; lacks
chestnut scapulars of
juvenile Western
Sandpiper. (See also
p. 16) New York,
mid-September. *RJC*

**Semipalmated
Sandpiper**
adult summer
Alaska, June. *R. van
Meurs*

**Semipalmated
Sandpiper**
adult winter Still
retains some worn,
faded summer wing-
coverts and tertials.
Florida, late
September. *RJC*

Western Sandpiper *Calidris mauri*

Migrant N American species; vagrant to W Europe.

Identification L15 (6″); WS30 (12″). Very small, with variable, but typically medium-length, slightly decurved black bill and medium-length black legs, giving general shape recalling miniature Dunlin. Partial webbing between toes. Primary projection beyond tertials very short. Sexes of similar size, but males are often noticeably shorter-billed. In flight from above, has a narrow white wing-bar and white sides to dark-centred rump; feet extend just beyond tail. Feeds both by picking and by probing, often wading quite deeply.

Juvenile Crown greyish, darker in centre; ear-coverts rather pale; clear white supercilium, contrasting with dark eye-stripe. Upperparts greyish, but with strong chestnut fringes on mantle and, especially, on upper scapulars; mantle and scapular Vs faint; dark anchor-shaped marks on rear lower scapulars (Fig. 7, p. 96).

First-winter/adult winter Uniformly grey above, crown finely streaked; below, white, with narrow band of fine streaking across upper breast. First-winter retains dark-centred, pale-fringed juvenile wing-coverts; adult has uniform grey wing-coverts.

Adult summer Rufous on crown, ear-coverts and at base of lower scapulars; extensive small chevron markings across breast and on flanks.

Call Thin, high-pitched 'jeet'.

Status, habitat and distribution Common, breeding on sub-arctic tundra in W Alaska and adjacent NE Siberia. On southward migration occurs along Atlantic coast south from Massachusetts; winters in California, and from New Jersey south to S America. Less common in spring on east coast of USA. Rare in E Canada; rare vagrant to Europe.

Racial variation No races recognized.

Similar species Confusion in N America most likely with Semipalmated Sandpiper; see also Dunlin, and Table 5, p. 100–101.

References Jonsson & Grant 1984; Veit & Jonsson 1984; Wallace 1980c.

Western Sandpiper
juvenile Aged by neat, pale-fringed upperparts and wing-coverts; note chestnut on scapulars. Long bill suggests a female. California, early September. *RJC*

Western Sandpiper
adult summer Attaining summer plumage; note diagnostic chevrons on underparts. Short bill suggests a male. Location and date not known. *D. Curry/ NHPA*

Western Sandpiper
adult winter This individual still retains traces of adult summer plumage, including a chevron on its flank; shortish bill suggests a male. New Jersey, late September. *RJC*

Rufous-necked Stint *Calidris ruficollis*

Vagrant to the N Atlantic area.

Identification L14.5 (5.75″); WS32 (12.5″). Very small, with short, straight, medium-length black bill and medium-length black legs. Toes unwebbed. Primary projection beyond tertials long. Has longest wings of any stint, giving attenuated profile to rear end. Plumages vary seasonally. Sexes of similar size. Flight pattern (p. 97) and manner of feeding as Little Stint.

Juvenile Head pattern plainer than that of Little Stint, supercilium duller, lacking obvious 'split' effect. Mantle and upper scapulars dark-centred with rufous fringes; indistinct off-white mantle *V*; lower scapulars have lozenge-shaped dark centre to tip (Fig. 7). Wing-coverts and tertials grey, with narrow, darker centres and whitish fringes.

First-winter/adult winter Generally similar to Little Stint, but rather more uniform and paler grey above. Has dark area from lores through eye to ear-coverts. Lacks breast-band. First-winter retains juvenile wing-coverts; those of adult are greyer and less worn.

First-summer Generally attains only partial summer plumage.

Adult summer Distinctive, with pale or white supercilium behind eye; face, throat and upper breast uniform bright orange or brick-red, bordered with a necklace of black streaks across lower breast. Broad rusty fringes to black-centred upper scapulars and some tertials; indistinct mantle *V*.

Call Similar to that of Little Stint.

Status, habitat and distribution Breeds on wet tundra in NE Siberia and (rarely) NW Alaska, wintering SE Asia to Australasia. Very rare vagrant to eastern USA and Europe.

Racial variation No races recognized.

Similar species Little Stint; see also Table 5, p. 100–101.

References Jonsson & Grant 1984; Veit & Jonsson 1984; Wallace 1980c.

Fig. 7. Lower rear scapulars of the juvenile stints/peeps (after Jonsson & Grant 1984)

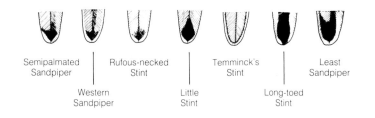

Semipalmated
Sandpiper

Rufous-necked
Stint

Temminck's
Stint

Least
Sandpiper

Western
Sandpiper

Little
Stint

Long-toed
Stint

Rufous-necked Stint
juvenile Note contrast between rufous upperparts and greyish wing-coverts and tertials. Japan, mid-September. *T. Shiota*

Rufous-necked Stint
adult winter Uniformly fresh plumage. The dark feather centres are usually obscured when the bird is standing normally. New Zealand, late November. *Brian Chudleigh*

Rufous-necked Stint
adult summer Note all-red chin and throat; summer Little Stint has white chin and throat. Japan, mid-May. *T. Shiota*

97

Little Stint *Calidris minuta*

A European and Asiatic migrant; vagrant to N America.

Identification L13 (5″); WS30 (12″). Very small, with medium-length, finely tipped, slightly decurved black bill, and medium-length black legs which may be brownish-black in juveniles. Toes unwebbed. Primary projection beyond tertials long. Plumages vary seasonally. Sexes of similar size. In flight from above, has a narrow white wing-bar and white sides to dark-centred rump. Feeds actively, picking from surface, occasionally wading.

Juvenile Crown has darker central area and a narrow white lateral stripe above and behind eye, giving a usually prominent split-supercilium effect. Dark-centred mantle and scapular feathers fringed rufous, except for prominent white mantle and scapular *V*s; lower rear scapulars have solid dark centres (Fig. 7, p. 96), but occasionally they resemble those of Rufous-necked Stint. Sides of upper breast neatly streaked over orange-buff wash.

First-winter/adult winter Grey above, but generally with feather centres darker, giving scalloped appearance at distance. Usually has uniform greyish wash, sometimes streaked, around upper breast. First-winter retains some worn juvenile wing-coverts, which are browner than the greyer, more uniform adult feathers.

Adult summer Head and breast variably orange-rufous with dark streaks and mottling below; chin and throat always white. Mantle, scapulars and wing-coverts dark brown, with broad orange to orange-rufous fringes; prominent mantle *V*.

Call High-pitched, staccato 'stit'.

Status, habitat and distribution Breeds on high-arctic coastal tundra in N Scandinavia (small numbers) and in N Russia and NW Asia. On migration and in winter uses muddy coastal and estuarine localities; winters mainly in Africa south of Sahara, but smaller numbers occur around Mediterranean and north to S England. Vagrant to eastern N America.

Racial variation No races recognized, but occasional 'grey-morph' juveniles occur which have less rufous, more uniformly coloured upperpart fringes, and mantle and scapular *V*s indistinct or absent.

Similar species Dark legs and lack of webbing between toes eliminate all other N Atlantic peeps/stints except Rufous-necked. In juvenile and summer plumages Little Stint can be separated by brownish coverts with rufous fringes; in winter doubtfully distinguished by darker feather centres and, when present, grey-washed breast-band. See also Table 5, p. 100–101.

References Jonsson & Grant 1984; Veit & Jonsson 1984; Wallace 1980c.

Little Stint
juvenile Aged by
dark-centred, rufous-
fringed upperparts;
note 'split
supercilium' and
mantle *V*. E England,
late August. *RJC*

Little Stint
juvenile A 'grey-
morph' individual,
lacking mantle *V* and
any rufous tinge to
upperparts.
E England, mid-
September. *RJC*

Little Stint
adult winter Aged
by uniformly worn
darkish-centred
upperparts and wing-
coverts. Gambia,
mid-January. *RJC*

Little Stint
adult summer In
fresh plumage; note
white chin and
throat. E England,
late April. *RJC*

Table 5. Comparison of the small *Calidris* species; note that the primary projection

Species	Main Structural Features	Juvenile Plumage
Semipalmated Sandpiper (black legs) (p. 92)	Shortish blunt-tipped bill; short primary projection; toes webbed.	Relatively uniform dull greyish upperparts, fringed paler.
Western Sandpiper (black legs) (p. 94)	Longish slightly decurved bill; very short primary projection; longish legs; toes webbed.	Rufous fringes on mantle and scapulars; coverts grey.
Rufous-necked Stint (black legs) (p. 96)	Shortish straight bill; long primary projection; elongated rear end; legs shortish; toes unwebbed.	Rufous fringes on mantle and scapulars; indistinct pale mantle *V*; coverts grey.
Little Stint (black legs) (p. 98)	Shortish slightly decurved bill; long primary projection; toes unwebbed.	Split supercilium; rufous fringes on upperparts and coverts; clear mantle and scapular *V*s.
Temminck's Stint (yellowish legs) (p. 102)	Slightly decurved bill; tail projects beyond primaries; shortish legs; white outer tail feathers.	Upperparts dull, with dark subterminal lines and pale fringes; breast brown.
Long-toed Stint (yellowish legs) (p. 104)	Slightly decurved bill; pale base to lower mandible; primary projection minimal; upright stance.	Split supercilium; mantle and scapulars fringed bright rufous; white covert fringes; breast sides streaked.
Least Sandpiper (yellowish legs) (p. 106)	Slightly decurved bill; primary projection minimal; bent-legged, crouching stance.	Diffuse supercilium; rufous-fringed upperparts; faint pale mantle '*V*'; breast uniformly streaked.

100

Little Stint
adult summer Has acquired a few greyish winter feathers on upperparts, but is still essentially in worn summer plumage. E England, mid-August. *RJC*

is that beyond the tertials

Winter Plumage	*Summer Plumage*
Coarsely streaked crown; breast streaked on sides only.	Dullish upperparts; strongly streaked breast and flanks.
Finely streaked crown; fine streaking across breast.	Rufous on crown and ear-coverts; small dark chevrons on breast and flanks.
Uniformly grey upperparts with dark shaft-streaks.	Entire face and throat uniform brick-red bordered below with streaked 'necklace'; indistinct mantle *V*.
Upperpart feathers have darker centres; grey washed breast-band.	Face and breast dark-streaked over orange-rufous wash; throat white; clear mantle *V*.
Dull uniform brownish upperparts; breast brown.	Random dark feathers in mantle and scapulars; breast brown.
Upperpart feathers have dark centres and broad greyish fringes.	Dark of forehead reaches bill; broad rufous, slightly scalloped tertial fringes; pale mantle *V*.
Uniform brown-grey upperparts.	Supercilia meet above bill; dull rufous fringes to tertials; breast coarsely streaked.

Temminck's Stint *Calidris temminckii*

A European and Asiatic migrant species.

Identification L14 (5.5"); WS31 (12"). Very small, with short, finely tipped, slightly decurved black bill and medium-length yellowish or greenish legs. Tail often extends beyond folded wings. A dull-plumaged stint with rather plain head (lacking obvious supercilium) and uniform brown upper breast in all plumages. Sexes of similar size. In flight from above (p. 198), shows narrow white wing-bar, white sides to dark-centred rump and, diagnostically among stints, white outer tail feathers (best seen on take-off and landing); feet do not extend beyond tail. Feeds by picking, often in crouched bent-legged stance, not infrequently among vegetation at edge of open mud.

Juvenile Uniformly plain buffish-grey upperparts, feathers having narrow, dark subterminal line and pale buff fringes, a pattern unique among the stints (Fig. 7, p. 96).

First-winter/adult winter Uniformly greyish-brown upperparts; breast (sometimes sides only) light brown. First-winter retains some worn juvenile wing-coverts.

Adult summer Mantle and scapulars irregularly blotched darker owing to random mixture of blackish-centred, pale-fringed feathers and uniform greyish ones. Prominence of supercilium varies among individuals, those with indistinct supercilium appearing plain-faced.

Call Distinctive thin, high-pitched trilling, often continuously repeated.

Status, habitat and distribution Breeds in arctic and sub-arctic regions, often near or among low vegetation, from Scotland (rare) and Norway continuously throughout N USSR. An uncommon migrant to W Europe, usually occurring singly or in small numbers in muddy freshwater environments, both near the coast and inland; vagrant in Ireland. Winters locally around the Mediterranean, and in Africa between the Sahara and the equator. No east N American records.

Racial variation No races recognized.

Similar species Yellowish legs are shared only with Least Sandpiper and the very rare Long-toed Stint (see also Table 5, p. 100–101); but white outer tail feathers, juvenile upperpart feathers and call are all diagnostic. In all plumages, Temminck's has a rather uniform brownish breast, which is white or sharply streaked in the other two species.

References Jonsson & Grant 1984; Veit & Jonsson 1984; Wallace 1980c.

Temminck's Stint
juvenile The dark submarginal lines on the upperpart feathers are unique among the stints/ peeps. Bulgaria, late August. *J. Lawton Roberts*

Temminck's Stint
adult summer Norway, late June. *Gordon Langsbury*

Long-toed Stint *Calidris subminuta*

Migrant Asiatic species; vagrant to W Europe.

Identification L13 (5.5″); WS29 (11.5″). Very small, with medium-length, slightly decurved black bill with pale base to lower mandible, and medium-length yellowish legs. Longer neck, longer legs and longer toes than other stints. Primaries project marginally beyond tertials. Sexes of similar size. In flight from above, is similar to Least Sandpiper, but toes extend just beyond tail. Feeds by picking, generally at freshwater margins, with rather upright stance.

Juvenile Crown rusty, streaked; contrasty, off-white supercilia do not meet on forehead; lateral crown-stripes give split-supercilium effect. Upperparts have dark feather centres with bright rufous fringes; obvious creamy mantle *V*; inner wing-coverts have white tips and fringes. Becomes much plainer above when worn. Elongated dark centre to lower scapulars reaches feather tip (Fig. 7, p. 96). Breast streaked over brownish wash, often paler and unstreaked at centre; remainder of underparts white.

First-winter/adult winter Head pattern as that of juvenile, but less contrasty. Upperparts generally brownish-grey, but have distinctive blackish feather centres, with broad grey-brown fringes to scapulars and wing-coverts. First-winter retains worn juvenile wing-coverts.

Adult summer Head pattern much as that of juvenile. Mantle and scapulars, inner wing-coverts and tertials blackish with broad rufous fringes; creamy mantle *V*. Breast finely streaked dark brown.

Call Soft, liquid 'chree' or disyllabic 'chuilp'.

Status, habitat and distribution Breeds near tree-line in marshy sub-arctic regions of E USSR, wintering in SE Asia and Australia. Very rare vagrant to W Europe; no eastern N American records.

Racial variation No races recognized.

Similar species Least Sandpiper (see also Table 5, p. 100–101); Temminck's Stint also has yellowish legs.

References Jonsson & Grant 1984; Veit & Jonsson 1984; Wallace 1980c.

Long-toed Stint
juvenile Note 'split supercilium', clear mantle *V*, and pale base to lower mandible; aged by bright, neatly fringed upperparts. N England, September. *Paul Doherty*

Long-toed Stint
juvenile In worn, dull plumage. Oman, date not known. *Conrad Greaves/ Aquila*

Least Sandpiper *Calidris minutilla*

A migrant N American species; vagrant to W Europe.

Identification L13 (5.5″); WS28 (11″). Very small, with medium-length, tapered, slightly decurved black bill and medium-length yellowish legs. Primary tips barely extend beyond tertials. Brownish in all plumages. Sexes of similar size. In flight from above (p. 198), shows narrow white wing-bar and white sides to dark-centred rump; feet do not project beyond tail. Feeds by picking with crouched stance.

Juvenile Crown rusty, streaked; dull supercilia meet on forehead. Upperparts have dark feather centres and bright rusty-brown fringes, and an inconspicuous creamy mantle *V*; elongated dark centre to lower scapulars (Fig. 7, p. 96). Breast uniformly streaked and washed brown; remainder of underparts white.

First-winter/adult winter Head pattern as that of juvenile but less contrasty. Uniformly brownish-grey above; breast streaked or washed brownish-grey; remainder of underparts white. First-winter loses some or all juvenile wing-coverts, so only those retaining juvenile buff (fading to off-white) covert fringes can be aged with confidence.

Adult summer Heavily streaked crown, rusty lores and ear-coverts; mantle and scapulars have blackish-brown centres, with broad pale brown-grey fringes when fresh; fringes quickly wear, revealing rusty feather bases. Creamy mantle *V*. Breast heavily streaked dark brown.

Call Very high-pitched 'kreet', with rising inflexion.

Status, habitat and distribution Common, breeding on wettish tundra or grassland near the tree-line, continuously from Alaska to Newfoundland; winters from N Carolina south to central S America.

Racial variation No races recognized.

Similar species Long-toed and Temminck's Stints; Table 5, p. 100–101.

References Jonsson & Grant 1984; Veit & Jonsson 1984; Wallace 1980c.

Least Sandpiper *juvenile* Aged by bright rusty, neatly fringed upperparts; legs and bill stained whitish. Note mantle *V*. Florida, late September. *RJC*

Least Sandpiper
first-winter Aged by
plain upperparts and
neatly pale-fringed
retained juvenile
wing-coverts and
tertials. California,
mid-September. *RJC*

Least Sandpiper
adult winter Aged
by uniformly brownish
upperparts, wing-
coverts and tertials.
Florida, mid-
September. *RJC*

Least Sandpiper
adult summer
Note completely
black bill at
all ages.
Alaska, early June.
R. van Meurs

White-rumped Sandpiper *Calidris fuscicollis*
N American long-distance migrant; vagrant to Europe.
Identification L16.5 (6.5"); WS38 (15"). Small, with medium-length, slightly decurved black bill (usually pale at base of lower mandible) and medium-length blackish legs. Long-winged, with wing-tips extending beyond tail. Sexes of similar size. In flight from above, has a narrow white wing-bar, narrow U-shaped white 'rump' (uppertail-coverts) and darker tail; feet do not extend beyond tail. Feeds with body held horizontally, picking from surface.
Juvenile Rusty crown, broad white supercilium; mantle and upper scapulars fringed rusty (except for whitish mantle and scapular *V*s); wing-coverts tipped whitish. Breast and flanks finely streaked grey; remainder of underparts white.
First-winter/adult winter Adults have brownish-grey upperparts, with darker centres to feathers of mantle and upper scapulars. First-winter retains some juvenile scapulars and wing-coverts until at least January. (Not usually seen in N America in these plumages.)
Adult summer White supercilium; streaked crown, ear-coverts and mantle, all with rusty tinge; dark-centred scapulars have grey, rusty and whitish fringes. Breast and flanks with bold dark streaks and chevrons.
Call A distinctive, thin, high-pitched 'tzeet'.
Status, habitat and distribution Common, breeding on wet, near-coastal tundra from N Alaska east through Canada to Southampton Island. Migrates south from Labrador through eastern N America, to winter in southern S America; returns through central USA. Outside breeding season favours muddy, near-coastal freshwater margins. Vagrant to Europe, most during July–October.
Racial variation No races recognized.
Similar species Larger than all the stints. Similar to Baird's Sandpiper, which is slightly smaller, has finer, straighter bill, is generally rusty-brown above in all plumages, and lacks the white uppertail-coverts. The only other white-rumped small sandpipers are Curlew Sandpiper and Stilt Sandpiper, both of which are slightly larger, longer-necked and longer-legged.

White-rumped Sandpiper
juvenile Aged by pale-fringed unworn upperparts and wing-coverts; note elongated body shape, wing-tips extending beyond tail, and pale base to lower mandible. New York, date not known. *T.H. Davis/ VIREO*

White-rumped Sandpiper
adult Moulting to adult winter; aged by combination of fresh grey mantle and scapulars, and worn wing-coverts and tertials. SW England, mid-October.
J.B. & S. Bottomley

Baird's Sandpiper *Calidris bairdii*

N American long-distance migrant; vagrant to Europe.

Identification L15 (6″); WS39 (15.5″). Very small, with straight, rather slender, medium-length blackish bill and medium-length blackish legs. Long-winged, with wing-tips extending beyond tail. Sexes of similar size. In flight from above (p. 198), shows a very narrow white wing-bar, a little white at sides of rump, and a dark-centred grey tail; feet do not extend beyond tail. Feeds with horizontal carriage, often on dry, sparsely vegetated areas, less often at water's edge, picking from surface.

Juvenile General appearance brown with rusty tinge. Streaked brown crown, indistinct supercilium; upperparts and wing-coverts brown, strongly scalloped with buffish or whitish feather fringes. Breast streaked brown over buff wash, usually forming clear-cut breast-band; remainder of underparts white.

First-winter/adult winter Uniformly mid-brown above, with indistinct supercilium; brown across breast. First-winter generally retains juvenile coverts. (Not usually seen in N America in these plumages.)

Adult summer Crown strongly streaked dark brown; mantle and scapulars dark brown/blackish with broad buff fringes. Breast heavily streaked dark brown.

Call A low 'treep'.

Status, habitat and distribution Breeds on dry tundra, both coastally and inland, in NE Siberia and from N Alaska eastwards to Baffin Island, Ellesmere Island and NW Greenland. Migrates south mainly through prairies, also returning through interior N America; uncommon in east N America, particularly in spring. Winters in central and southern S America. Vagrant to W Europe, nearly all records being in August–October.

Racial variation No races recognized, but rarely individuals of all ages may be noticeably greyer than usual.

Similar species See White-rumped Sandpiper for separation from that species. A little larger than the stints. Distinguished from Dunlin by smaller size, finer bill, primary extension beyond tail, and less conspicuous wing-bar; browner and more scaly in juvenile plumage, lacks adult summer Dunlin's black belly.

References Haig 1983; Marchant 1985.

Baird's Sandpiper
juvenile Aged by strongly scalloped, brownish upperparts; note elongated profile, wing-tips extending beyond tail, and slender all-black bill. Wyoming, mid-September.
R. Pop

Baird's Sandpiper
adult summer
Alaska, June. *R. van Meurs*

Baird's Sandpiper
adult Moulting to adult winter; upperparts are being replaced by fresh winter feathers, but this individual still retains worn wing-coverts and tertials. Ireland, mid-September. *Richard T. Mills*

Pectoral Sandpiper *Calidris melanotos*

Asiatic and N American long-distance migrant; vagrant to Europe.

Identification Male L23 (9"); WS44 (17.5"). Female L21 (8"); WS40 (16"). Medium-sized or small, with long neck; medium-length, slightly decurved brownish bill, darker at tip; medium-length yellowish legs. Streaked breast has abrupt junction with white belly. Males rather larger than females. In flight from above (p. 198), uniform except for a very narrow white wing-bar and white sides to dark-centred rump and uppertail-coverts; underwing whitish; feet just reach tail-tip. Feeds among vegetation and at muddy freshwater margins; picks from surface and occasionally probes.

Juvenile Crown streaked; whitish supercilium; dark brown upperparts with rusty feather fringes, except for whitish mantle and scapular Vs and off-white wing-covert fringes. Rusty fringes have a bright appearance, but bird becomes greyer as fringes fade and wear. Brown-streaked foreneck and breast; remainder of underparts white.

First-winter/adult winter Head pattern much as that of juvenile, though less rusty; upperparts greyish, with dark feather centres and broad paler fringes. First-winter may retain some rusty-fringed wing-coverts and tertials. Juveniles moult only in winter quarters, adults mostly so, hence this plumage not generally seen in N America.

First-summer May show mixture of adult-type winter and summer upperpart feathers.

Adult summer Like juvenile, but duller, with inconspicuous supercilium; mantle and scapulars have broader buff or off-white fringes. Breast of male is dark, and mottled or spotted, that of female streaked brown over brownish wash.

Call A low, slightly rasping 'krrick'.

Status, habitat and distribution Breeds on low-lying, poorly drained tundra, from 105°E in N Siberia to N Alaska, and in N Canada west from Hudson Bay. Most migrate to southern S America, through N America and over W Atlantic; returns north through interior N America in spring. Commonest N American vagrant to W Europe, mostly in August–October, but there are records throughout year.

Racial variation No races recognized.

Similar species Sharp-tailed Sandpiper *C. acuminata* (L19 (8"), WS41 (16")), a scarce vagrant to both sides of N Atlantic. Sharp-tailed has similar general character and colour, but has slightly shorter legs and is 'pot-bellied'; in all plumages it has diffuse lower margin to streaked breast, and has whiter supercilium. Juvenile Sharp-tailed is generally more rufous, with rusty cap, rufous wash on breast, and white eye-ring; summer adults have bold chevrons on breast and flanks.

References Britton 1980; Kieser & Smith 1982.

Pectoral Sandpiper
juvenile Aged by neatly fringed upperparts and wing-coverts; note strongly streaked breast and mantle *V.* New Jersey, mid-September. *RJC*

Pectoral Sandpiper
first-winter Duller upperparts and retained rufous-fringed juvenile greater coverts and tertials indicate first-winter. New Zealand, late March. *Brian Chudleigh*

Pectoral Sandpiper
adult summer Displaying male. Alaska, date not known. *J.P. Myers/ VIREO*

Curlew Sandpiper *Calidris ferruginea*

Occurs in W Europe as a migrant; vagrant to N America.

Identification L20 (8″); WS41 (16″). Small, with longish neck, long, decurved black bill and medium-length black legs. Plumages vary seasonally. Sexes of similar size. In flight from above (p. 198), has a white wing-bar and white lower rump and uppertail-coverts; underwing white; feet extend just beyond tail. Feeds by picking from mud, but also often wades quite deeply.

Juvenile Streaked darkish crown, prominent whitish supercilium; greyish-brown upperparts (mantle and upper scapulars dark brown) and wing-coverts, with dark subterminal lines and narrow whitish fringes. Breast lightly streaked and washed pale salmon-buff; remainder of underparts white.

First-winter/adult winter Grey crown, prominent white supercilium; grey upperparts and wing-coverts, with dark shaft-streaks and narrow white fringes; grey flecks across breast, otherwise underparts white. First-winter can be distinguished by retained worn juvenile wing-coverts. (Uncommon in Europe in these plumages.)

First-summer Attains adult winter-type plumage or has a scattering of adult summer mantle, scapular or underpart feathers. (Not normally seen north of the Mediterranean in this plumage.)

Adult summer Crown streaked; supercilium faint; mantle and scapulars blackish, with fairly broad greyish feather tips; face, nape, neck and underparts brick-red, though vent and undertail-coverts are variably brick-red or white. In breeding pairs, female may perhaps be distinguished by slightly longer bill and scattered white fringes on underparts; body moult during spring and autumn makes the latter feature valueless for sexing migrants.

Call A quiet 'chirrup'.

Status, habitat and distribution Breeds on tundra with scattered ponds in N USSR between 80° and 150°E. Fairly common in W Europe on southerly migration to winter in W Africa (occasional individuals winter in W Europe), but scarce in spring as return migration is via C Europe; also moves directly south overland, to winter in remainder of Africa, S Asia and Australasia. Vagrant to Iceland and Spitsbergen, and along east N American coast south to Virginia.

Racial variation No races recognized.

Similar species Dunlin; Stilt Sandpiper shares white lower rump/uppertail-coverts, but lacks wing-bar and has thicker-tipped, less decurved bill and longer yellow or greenish legs.

Curlew Sandpiper
juvenile Aged by neat, pale-fringed upperparts and wing-coverts; note pale supercilium and uniformly decurved bill. E England, early September. *RJC*

Curlew Sandpiper
first-winter Aged by contrast of fresh upperparts and worn wing-coverts. Gambia, mid-January. *RJC*

Curlew Sandpiper
adult summer In fresh summer plumage; pale tips and fringes will later wear, making bird darker; white on bill is staining. New Zealand, late March. *Brian Chudleigh*

Purple Sandpiper *Calidris maritima*

A migrant which occurs on both sides of the N Atlantic.

Identification L21 (8″); WS41 (16″). Small, plump and short-necked, with medium-length, slightly decurved blackish bill with yellowish base, and short yellow legs. Sexes of similar size. In flight from above, (p. 199), is rather dark with white wing-bar and narrow white sides to dark-centred rump; feet do not project beyond tail. Feeds in rather leisurely manner on intertidal rocks; uncommon in other habitats.

Juvenile Crown has rusty tinge; faint supercilium; mantle and scapulars dark grey, fringed rufous and whitish; wing-coverts and tertials dark grey with neat off-white fringes. Upper breast heavily streaked greyish, lower breast and flanks sparsely streaked and spotted.

First-winter/adult winter Head, mantle and scapulars uniformly dark grey, the latter having a purplish sheen. Wing-coverts have diffuse fringes; first-winter retains juvenile wing-coverts. Underparts much as juvenile.

First-summer As adult summer, but retains worn juvenile wing-coverts.

Adult summer Crown dark brown; buff supercilium; mantle and scapulars blackish, with broad buff fringes; breast, upper belly and flanks heavily streaked greyish-brown.

Call 'Weet, wit', given in flight.

Status, habitat and distribution Breeds on lichen-rich tundra in Canadian arctic islands, Greenland, Iceland, Scotland (rare), Spitsbergen, Norway, and N USSR to 110°E. Winters on rocky coasts from Newfoundland to Carolinas, in Iceland, and from N Finland south to Portugal.

Racial variation No races recognized.

Similar species Dumpy shape and short, yellowish legs are distinctive, even away from usual rocky habitat. The very closely related Rock Sandpiper *C. ptilocnemus* of the Pacific coast has not been recorded in eastern N America.

Purple Sandpiper
juvenile Aged by
neat, pale-fringed
dark upperparts.
E England, August.
Roger Tidman

Purple Sandpiper
adult winter Aged
by uniformly toned
upperparts and wing-
coverts. Note more
contrasty wing-covert
fringes of first-winter,
Frontispiece.
E England, early
April. *RJC*

Purple Sandpiper
adult summer In
worn plumage; aged
by contrast between
bright dark
upperparts and dull,
worn wing-coverts.
N Wales, early
August. *RJC*

Dunlin *Calidris alpina*

A widespread migrant, occurring on both sides of N Atlantic.

Identification L19 (7.5"); WS34 (13.5"). Small (though can be variable in size), with medium or long, slightly decurved black bill and medium-length black legs. Folded primaries typically just reach tail-tip, and extend a short distance beyond tertials. In flight from above (p. 199), brown-grey with narrow white wing-bar and dark-centred white rump; feet just reach tail-tip. Feeds with hunched, short-necked stance, by picking and probing to shallow depth, often with rapid vibration of bill and head; commonly wades.

Juvenile Rather rufous-toned head and breast, with brownish crown; upperparts darkish brown with rusty fringes, often with pale mantle V. Breast, upper belly and flanks strongly streaked or spotted; remainder of underparts white.

First-winter/adult winter Brownish-grey upperparts; crown and, particularly, tertials and primaries darker. Foreneck and breast diffusely streaked grey; remainder of underparts white. First-winter retains neat pale-fringed juvenile wing-coverts and tertials; those of adults appear more uniform.

First-summer/adult summer Bright, rusty or chestnut, fringes to blackish-centred feathers of crown and upperparts; brownish-streaked neck and breast, black belly, and white vent and undertail-coverts. Males of most races show whiter hindneck than females. First-summer can be distinguished by well-worn, pale-fringed wing-coverts; sometimes only partially acquires summer plumage.

Call 'Treep', often given at take-off and in flight.

Status, habitat and distribution Common throughout area, breeding on tussocky, hummocky tundra and moorland. Four N Atlantic races. In N America *C. a. hudsonia* breeds in arctic Canada west of Hudson Bay, occurring on passage and in winter along the east coast from Massachusetts to Florida and the Gulf Coast. In Europe *C. a. arctica* breeds in NE Greenland, migrating through Iceland, Britain, Ireland and W France, probably wintering in NW Africa; *C. a. alpina* breeds in Norway and N USSR, migrating via Norway and the Baltic, wintering in the British Isles and France; *C. a. schinzii* breeds in S Greenland, Iceland, the British Isles and around the Baltic, wintering in NW Africa.

Racial variation Adult summer *alpina* can in favourable conditions be distinguished from *arctica* and *schinzii* (see Table 6), particularly when direct comparison is possible. Feather wear later in the season often renders the distinctions less obvious, upperparts becoming dull and blackish. In winter plumage, flanks of *hudsonia* are more streaked than those of other N Atlantic races.

Similar species Black belly of adult summer Dunlin is diagnostic in N Atlantic. Western Sandpiper is smaller, often shorter-billed, appearing proportionally larger-headed and shorter-bodied. Baird's Sandpiper is smaller, shorter-billed, with folded wings projecting beyond tail-tip. Curlew Sandpiper is longer-necked, longer-legged, has distinctive juvenile and adult summer plumages, and has a white rump in flight. Broad-billed Sandpiper is shorter-legged, with a distinctive double supercilium.

References Clark 1987; Ferns & Green 1979; Greenwood 1984.

Table 6. Distinctions between N Atlantic races of Dunlin in summer (after Prater *et al.* 1977)

Race	Mantle/scapular fringes	Breast streaking	Belly patch
hudsonia	very bright chestnut	faint	large
arctica	grey/white to buffish	faint	small
schinzii	yellowish-red	heavy	small
alpina	rich chestnut	heavy	large

Dunlin

juvenile Aged by neatly fringed upperparts, and streaked and spotted breast and belly; this individual has acquired a few greyish winter scapulars.
E England, early September. *RJC*

Dunlin

first-winter Aged by mixture of greyish upperparts and neatly fringed, brownish juvenile wing-coverts and tertials, and all-white belly. Race *hudsonia*. New York, mid-September. *RJC*

Dunlin

first-winter Three worn tertials show this to be a first-winter individual; at this stage ageing becomes more difficult. Note streaked flanks, characteristic of race *hudsonia*. Florida, mid-January. *RJC*

Dunlin
first-summer A
mixture of adult
winter and summer-
type scapulars, and
heavily worn wing-
coverts. E England,
early May. *RJC*

Dunlin
adult summer In
fresh plumage;
whitish nape
indicates a male.
E England, early
May. *RJC*

Dunlin
adult summer
Female (brownish
nape) in worn
summer plumage.
E England, mid-
June. *RJC*

Broad-billed Sandpiper *Limicola falcinellus*

A European and Asiatic migrant species.

Identification L17 (7″); WS33 (13″). Small, short-necked, with long, slightly decurved blackish bill which is flattened horizontally and kinked downwards at the tip, and short greyish-black legs. In all plumages has a double supercilium which joins at forehead. Sexes of similar size. In flight from above, shows a blackish leading edge to the wing and a narrow white wing-bar; white at sides of blackish-centred rump; feet do not extend beyond tail. Feeds by gentle, vertical probing in mud or shallow water.

Juvenile Crown brown, with creamy double supercilium; mantle and scapulars dark brown with rufous-buff fringes and prominent cream mantle and scapular *V*s; wing-coverts dark brown, fringed buff. Breast and flanks streaked brown; remainder of underparts white.

First-winter/adult winter Crown greyish; whitish double supercilium; upperparts uniformly dull grey, feathers tipped off-white with darker shaft-streaks; wing-coverts of adult as upperparts, but with fairly broad off-white fringes. First-winter retains dark juvenile wing-coverts. Dark fore-wing may show at bend of folded wing, as in winter Sanderling.

First-summer/adult summer Similar to juvenile, initially with whitish fringes to upperparts giving 'frosty' appearance; these soon wear, at first revealing bright rufous-buff fringes to otherwise blackish mantle and scapulars, but further wear renders upperparts very dark; mantle and scapular *V*s generally obvious. Upper breast and flanks heavily spotted; remainder of underparts white.

Call A trilled, almost buzzing 'chrreet'.

Status, habitat and distribution Uncommon, breeding in extensive marshland in the boreal forest zone. *L. f. falcinellus* breeds from Norway to NW USSR and migrates southeast to winter in E Africa, and thus is rare in W Europe; *L. f. sibirica* breeds discontinuously through N Siberia, wintering in S and SE Asia and Australia. No east N American records.

Racial variation In adult summer plumage *sibirica* has brighter, less black and more rufous upperparts, but is most unlikely to occur in N Atlantic area at this time; upperparts of fresh juvenile *sibirica* have broader buff fringes; races probably indistinguishable in winter.

Similar species In all plumages distinguished from Dunlin by double supercilium, bill shape and short, non-black legs; in juvenile and adult summer plumages by lack of Dunlin's breast spots or belly patch respectively. From Jack Snipe by kinked (not straight) bill, much less rufous coloration, and greyish-black legs.

Broad-billed Sandpiper
juvenile Neatly fringed upperparts with prominent mantle *V*. Netherlands, early September.
P. de Knijff

Broad-billed Sandpiper
adult winter An individual of race *sibirica* (identified from locality), slightly paler and greyer than nominate *falcinellus* in winter. W Australia, mid-September. *Brian Chudleigh*

Broad-billed Sandpiper
adult summer Finland, early June.
R. Pop

Stilt Sandpiper *Micropalama himantopus*

N American long-distance migrant; vagrant to Europe.

Identification L20 (8″); WS41 (16″). Small, with long neck and long, slightly decurved black bill and long yellowish or greenish legs. Brownish or greyish above; underparts pale, except adult summer which is heavily barred beneath. Sexes of similar size. In flight from above, is uniform apart from white rump and tail-coverts; feet extend beyond tail. Feeds by vertical probing in both mud and water, often wading to belly.

Juvenile Crown streaked, tinged rusty; whitish supercilium; mantle dark, with rufous and whitish fringes; scapulars and wing-coverts darkish, with whitish fringes. Neck and breast lightly streaked brown; remainder of underparts white. Legs often yellow.

First-winter/adult winter Generally greyish, including crown; white supercilium; upperpart feathers narrowly fringed whitish. First-winter retains tertials and replaces only some of juvenile wing-coverts, and these only from November, so darker-centred or worn tertials and wing-coverts indicate first-winter.

First-summer Much as adult winter.

Adult summer Crown rufous with dark streaks; whitish supercilium. Lores and ear-coverts bright rufous. Mantle and scapulars blackish, with broad buffish and whitish fringes; some dark barring on rump and uppertail-coverts; neck and upper breast heavily streaked blackish. Underparts from lower breast to undertail-coverts heavily barred blackish. Legs usually olive-green.

Call A monosyllabic 'querp'.

Status, habitat and distribution Breeds in sub-arctic region just north of tree-line, in a variety of habitats, from N Alaska east to Hudson Bay. Most migrate south through prairies, but some along Atlantic coast south from S Ontario. A few winter in Florida and on Gulf Coast, but most in central S America. Return migration almost entirely through interior N America. Rare vagrant to Europe, mainly during July–October.

Racial variation No races recognized.

Similar species Distinguished from Curlew Sandpiper by longer yellowish or greenish legs, lack of wing-bar, and barred underparts of adult summer. Grey-tailed Tattler *Heteroscelus brevipes* (call 'weet-eat'; L25 (10″), WS51 (20″)) of E Asia and Wandering Tattler *H. incanus* (call 'peet', rapidly repeated about ten times; L27 (11″), WS54 (21″)) of Pacific are the only other comparable species with barred underparts in summer; both are medium-sized, grey above in all plumages, have medium-length straight bills, short yellow legs, and lack white rump.

Reference Paulson 1986.

Stilt Sandpiper
juvenile Aged by neat, pale-fringed upperparts and wing-coverts. New York, date not known.
Urban Olsson

Stilt Sandpiper
first-winter Retains pale-fringed juvenile wing-coverts. Florida, mid-January. *RJC*

Stilt Sandpiper
adult summer
Alaska, June. *R. van Meurs*

Buff-breasted Sandpiper *Tryngites subruficollis*

N American long-distance migrant; vagrant to W Europe.

Identification L19 (7.5″); WS41 (16″). Small, long-necked, with small rounded head; short, fine, straight black bill and medium-length yellow or yellow-ochre legs. Crown has fine dark streaking; plain face, with prominent dark eye; upperparts scaly; face, neck and underparts buff. Males are 5% or so larger than females, and can, with care, be separated in the field. In flight, is uniform above, with primaries and secondaries slightly darker; below, strikingly white underwing contrasts with buff body; feet extend just beyond tail. Feeds, by picking, usually in short grassland, with rather hunched stance.

Juvenile Mantle and scapulars dark brown or blackish with contrasting narrow whitish fringes; wing-coverts have brown centres, dark subterminal marks and broader, less contrasting buff fringes.

First-winter This species probably has a complete post-juvenile moult, but, since this is not completed until spring, first-winter can be aged by retained juvenile wing-coverts.

First-summer/adult summer/adult winter These plumages are apparently indistinguishable. Head and underparts much as juvenile; mantle and scapulars dark-centred, with fairly broad, buff fringes; wing-coverts similar, but with less dark centres.

Call A quiet, trilled 'pr-r-r-reet'; generally rather silent.

Status, habitat and distribution Breeds on well-drained grassy tundra, locally in N Alaska and N Canada east to King William Island. Most migrate south through central USA, but some via Great Lakes to Massachusetts/New Jersey, then by direct flight over Atlantic to S America. Winters Argentina and Paraguay. Returns via central USA. Vagrant to Europe, most during mid-August to mid-October.

Racial variation No races recognized.

Similar species Most likely confusion is with juvenile Ruff, but is always smaller than the smallest female Ruff, has shorter, straighter and finer bill, yellow legs, and is buff beneath as far as the undertail-coverts.

Buff-breasted Sandpiper
juvenile Smaller scapulars and darker-centred wing-coverts than adult. SW England, early September. *RJC*

Buff-breasted Sandpiper
adult Alaska, June. *R. van Meurs*

Ruff *Philomachus pugnax*

A European and Asiatic migrant; may breed in Canada.

Identification Male L29 (11.5"); WS59 (23"). Female (Reeve) L22 (9"); WS47 (18.5"). Medium-sized, with long neck, smallish head, medium-length, slightly decurved bill, and medium-length legs. Colours of plumage and bare parts vary tremendously (but systematically) with age and sex, adult summer male having ear-tufts and uniquely long neck feathers ('ruff'); both bill and legs are variably dark or yellow/orange. Male is about 20% larger than female, with proportionately slightly shorter bill and longer legs; in Europe, a useful comparison species is Common Redshank, which is slightly smaller and shorter-legged than most males but larger than female. In flight looks 'humpbacked'; above (p. 199), has white wing-bar of variable extent and a white oval area on each side of dark-centred rump; feet project beyond tail. Feeds by picking in muddy areas, often among vegetation; sometimes wades.

Juvenile Plain head, with streaked crown and indistinct buff supercilium; upperparts very scaly, with blackish-brown feather centres and narrow pale buff fringes; often shows mantle *V*. Wing-covert feather centres are variable, solidly dark brown or dark brown patterned buff, but always have a buff fringe. Breast dull buff; remainder of underparts white. Bill blackish, with brownish base; legs dull yellowish-green.

First-winter Much as juvenile, but crown and hindneck greyish-brown; upperparts as adult winter, though a variable number of worn juvenile wing-coverts and tertials are retained. Legs as juvenile, or greenish, mottled yellow/orange.

First-summer May have similar plumage to adult summer, or, particularly those remaining in wintering area, only scattered summer feathers on upperparts. Leg colour as first-winter.

Adult winter Crown and hindneck dull brown; upperparts greyish-brown, feathers having darker centres and diffuse pale fringes. Incomplete, narrow white eye-ring; often also has whitish feathering at base of bill. Throat and foreneck white, greyish wash across breast;

remainder of underparts white. Base of bill may be orange; legs often yellowish or dull orange. A few individuals, generally males, have entire head and neck white.

Adult summer *Male*: In May–June acquires ruff and ear-tufts, and feathering of forehead and around eye is lost to reveal orange area of warty skin; remainder of summer plumage is attained earlier and retained longer. Individuals are very variable: ruff and ear-tufts (also mantle, scapulars and tertials) may be black, white, rufous, chestnut, etc., uniformly coloured, spotted or barred white, buff or rusty; belly often black, but variable. Bill usually dark-tipped and orange-based, but may be wholly dark or wholly orange; legs orange. *Female*: Head and hindneck streaked dark brown; mantle, scapulars and tertials typically brown, plain or patterned/barred rusty, fringed buff, but variable, occasionally having extensive pale markings, thus appearing much brighter than usual. Foreneck and breast generally brown, but may be patterned as upperparts. Bill usually dark, but may have orange at base; legs orange.

Call Usually silent.

Status, habitat and distribution Common, breeding in damp areas of low vegetation discontinuously from England (occasionally) and Netherlands north to N Scandinavia, N USSR and Asia. On migration and in winter generally frequents muddy freshwater areas. Small numbers winter from England and Netherlands south to the Mediterranean, the majority in Africa south of the Sahara; females tend to move further south than males. May breed in N Canada; vagrant or rare migrant in N America.

Racial variation No races recognized.

Similar species Outside breeding season, Buff-breasted Sandpiper.

References Chandler 1987c; Prater 1982; Reynolds 1984.

Ruff
juvenile A typical individual, with dark-centred, buff-fringed wing-coverts.
E England, mid-August. *RJC*

Ruff
juvenile A less usual variety, with reduced dark centres on wing-covert feathers. N Wales, mid-August. *RJC*

Ruff
adult winter E England, mid-August. *RJC*

Ruff
adult summer A typical female, but greenish legs suggest that this may be a first-summer individual. E England, early July. *RJC*

Ruff
adult summer A
strongly marked
female; orange legs
are typical of
summer adults.
E England, early
July. *RJC*

Ruff
adult summer
Displaying male in
full breeding
plumage. N Sweden,
June. *D.A. Smith*

Ruff
adult summer Male
moulting out of full
breeding plumage.
E England, early
July. *RJC*

Common Snipe (Snipe) *Gallinago gallinago*

A migrant or sedentary species, occurring on both sides of N Atlantic.

Identification L26 (10"); WS41 (16.5"). Medium-sized, bulky, with very long, straight, black-tipped brown bill and short dull yellow legs. Dark brown crown, creamy crown-stripe and broad supercilium; dark eye-stripe. Upperparts dark brown, with longitudinal creamy stripes on mantle and scapulars; tertials barred dark brown and rusty. Wing-coverts duller and paler, tipped or fringed buff. Foreneck and breast streaked dark brown with buff wash; flanks barred; remainder of underparts white. In flight, bill is held tilted downwards; from above (p. 199), dark, with narrow white trailing edge to secondaries; feet project just beyond tail. Feeds in mud by rapid, repeated, vertical probing; often wades up to belly.

Juvenile Wing-coverts (particularly inner medians) uniformly fringed pale buff with black subterminal line (Fig. 8).

First-winter/adult Tips of wing-coverts have dark line down shaft separating two oval cream spots. Post-juvenile moult includes wing-coverts; once these are replaced, first-winter and adult become indistinguishable. Adult shows no seasonal variation.

Call A rasping 'scaap' when flushed.

Status, habitat and distribution Fairly common, breeding in fresh-water marshes. *G. g. gallinago* breeds in Europe north from Portugal and Spain to N Scandinavia and N USSR, and *G. g. faeroeensis* in Orkney, Shetland, Faeroes and Iceland; both races winter from Denmark, Britain and Ireland to Africa south of Sahara. *G. g. delicata* breeds throughout N America north of about 43°N, wintering from 40°N south to northern S America.

Racial variation Compared with *gallinago, faeroeensis* is darker, with more rufous upperparts and narrower mantle and scapular stripes; *delicata* is even darker, less rufous, with breast and underwing more extensively barred. A very rare black morph, 'Sabine's Snipe', has been recorded both in Europe and in N America.

Similar species Great Snipe is bulkier, more extensively barred beneath, and has proportionately shorter bill; in flight, has dark, white-bordered panel on secondaries and white outer tail. Eurasian Woodcock has greater bulk, transverse bars on crown, and all-dark underparts. American Woodcock is of similar size to Common Snipe, but has transverse bars on crown and is rufous beneath.

Fig. 8. Common Snipe, inner median coverts: (a) juvenile, and (b) adult

(a)   (b)

Common Snipe
juvenile Aged by broad creamy tips to inner median coverts. E England, mid-September. *RJC*

Common Snipe
adult Aged by twin creamy ovals at tips of inner median coverts. (See also p. 17) E England, late July. *RJC*

Common Snipe
juvenile Showing lightly barred underwing characteristic of European race *gallinago;* N American race has heavily barred underwing. E England, mid-September. *RJC*

Jack Snipe *Lymnocryptes minimus*

A migrant European and Asiatic species; vagrant to N America.

Identification L18 (7"); WS34 (13.5"). Small, with long, pale-based, dark-tipped bill and short yellowish legs. Similar plumages at all ages. Dark crown; creamy double supercilium; dark eye-stripe; upperparts brownish, with prominent creamy scapular 'lines'. Breast and flanks streaked; remainder of underparts white. Sexes of similar size. In flight from above (p. 199), dark, with scapular lines prominent and thin white wing-bar; white trailing edge to secondaries; dark pointed tail; darkish beneath, with paler underwing-coverts; legs often folded under body. Feeds in muddy areas with horizontal stance and bobbing action, flexing legs repeatedly.

Age There appear to be no characters by which this species may be aged in the field.

Call Usually silent when flushed.

Status, habitat and distribution Scarce, breeding in swamps in N Scandinavia, N USSR and Asia. Winters in freshwater wetlands in Denmark, Britain and Ireland, southwards to C Africa. Very rare vagrant to Labrador.

Racial variation No races recognized.

Similar species Broad-billed Sandpiper.

Jack Snipe
There are no known features by which this species may be aged in the field. E England, February. *Roger Tidman*

Great Snipe *Gallinago media*

A European migrant; vagrant to N America.

Identification L28 (11″); WS45 (18″). Medium-sized, with bulky body, very long dark brown bill with pale yellow base, and short greenish or yellowish legs. Dark brown crown, creamy crown-stripe and broad supercilium; dark eye-stripe obvious on lores, but indistinct on ear-coverts. Upperparts dark brown, with longitudinal creamy stripes on mantle and scapulars; wing-coverts broadly tipped white, forming two prominent bars on folded wing. Throat and breast heavily spotted; most of belly, vent and undertail-coverts barred. Sexes of similar size. In flight (p. 200), bill is held near horizontal; above, is dark, with white-bordered dark panel on greater coverts; tail has prominent white sides and tip, most obvious at take-off and landing; feet do not extend beyond tail. Feeds by picking as well as by vertical probing.

Juvenile More rufous above than adult, but soon fades; wing-coverts tipped off-white or buff, less broadly than on adult; brown markings on white outer tail.

First-winter/adult Wing-coverts have broad white tips; outer tail white. Post-juvenile moult includes wing-coverts and tail; then first-winter and adult indistinguishable. Adult shows no seasonal variation.

Call Generally silent, but may give low croak when flushed.

Status, habitat and distribution Breeds in damp boreal woodland in Scandinavia and in USSR between 50° and 67°N; probably moves southwards through C Europe, as is a scarce migrant in W Europe; most winter in Africa south of Sahara.

Racial variation No races recognized.

Similar species Common Snipe.

References Wallace 1980d, e.

Great Snipe
juvenile Has already acquired adult-type wing-coverts with broad white tips, but retains juvenile outer tail feathers with dark markings. Israel, September. *Hadoram Shirihai*

Short-billed Dowitcher *Limnodromus griseus*

N American migrant; vagrant to Europe.

Identification L27 (10.5″); WS45 (17.5″). Medium-sized, with long (male) or very long (female), straight, pale-based and blackish-tipped bill, and medium-length dull yellow or yellowish-green legs. Darkish cap, prominent supercilium and dark eye-stripe; both upperparts and underparts show considerable seasonal variation. Barred tail usually has white bars as wide as or wider than dark ones (this criterion does not apply to the tail-coverts, which are more evenly barred). Sexes of similar size, but female generally has slightly longer bill. In flight from above (p. 200), fairly uniformly darkish (including rump), with white extending from upper rump in V up back; feet extend beyond tail. Feeds, usually in water and often in flocks, by rapidly probing bill vertically in mud; prefers brackish or saline water.

Juvenile Dark brown crown, broad off-white supercilium; mantle, scapulars and tertials dark brown, with bright buff fringes and internal markings ('tiger stripes') particularly on tertials. Breast buffish, spotted brown at sides; remainder of underparts largely white.

First-winter/adult winter Grey crown, off-white supercilium; upperparts uniformly grey; grey upper breast, often streaked and spotted, and with irregular, spotted lower margin; some darker grey spotting at breast sides. First-winter retains some distinctive juvenile scapulars and tertials, and many worn wing-coverts; can often be distinguished throughout winter.

First-summer Non-breeding birds may show only partial breeding plumage.

Adult summer Depends on race (see Table 7). Crown dark brown; reddish supercilium. Mantle feathers black-centred with rufous or pinkish-brown fringes; scapulars and tertials black, barred buff, with paler fringes. Underparts have orange-red or brownish-red base colour; breast spotted dark brown, flanks with brown spots and bars, belly variably orange-red to white.

Call A mellow, quick 'tu-tu-tu', recalling Ruddy Turnstone's rattle.

Status, habitat and distribution Common, breeding in three distinct areas in sub-arctic coniferous forest and muskeg: in S Alaska (*L. g. caurinus*), betwen about 55° and 62°N from British Columbia east to Hudson Bay (*L. g. hendersoni*), and in N Quebec and Labrador (*L. g. griseus*). Only the last two races occur along Atlantic coast on migration (*griseus* being the more numerous, particularly north of New Jersey), wintering from N Carolina south to Brazil. Very rare vagrant to Europe.

Racial variation Juvenile *caurinus* has narrower fringes to upperpart feathers, thus appearing darker than other two races; otherwise distinguishable only in adult summer plumage, when in general *caurinus* is intermediate between the other two races; see Table 7.

Similar species Long-billed Dowitcher is very slightly larger, and lacks the pale internal patterning of upperpart feathers in juvenile plumage, appearing in comparison rather dark; doubtfully distinguishable in winter by more extensive grey on breast, less spotted at margin; summer Long-billed most resembles *hendersoni*, with darkish all-red underparts, densely spotted foreneck and barred upper breast. Dowitchers with longest bills are female Long-billed. Except when diagnostic juvenile feathers can be seen, identification should always be confirmed by call.

References Nisbet 1980; Wallace 1980a; Wilds & Newlon 1983.

Table 7.   Distinguishing features of races of adult summer Short-billed Dowitchers

Race	Mantle and scapular fringes	Breast markings	Belly
caurinus	narrow	fairly heavily spotted	small white area
griseus	narrow	densely spotted and barred; flanks barred	mainly white, usually with dark spots
hendersoni	broad	moderately to lightly spotted; flanks usually have little barring	white area limited or absent

Short-billed Dowitcher
juvenile Internal yellowish markings on upperpart feathers, especially tertials, are diagnostic. Florida, mid-September. *RJC*

Short-billed Dowitcher
adult winter Aged by uniform upperparts and wing-coverts; in this plumage, lacks Long-billed's grey breast. Short bill suggests a male. (See also *first-winter*, p. 28) Florida, mid-January. *RJC*

Short-billed Dowitcher
adult summer Barred flanks suggest race *griseus.* Ontario, May. *Stephen J. Krasemann/NHPA*

Long-billed Dowitcher*
juvenile Aged and identified by neatly fringed, plain dark upperparts and tertials; long bill suggests a female. California, mid-September. *RJC*

*Note: Text follows.

Long-billed Dowitcher
adult winter Aged by uniform upper-parts and wing-coverts; broad dark bars on tail and more grey on breast indicate a Long-billed Dowitcher, as opposed to a Short-billed. California, mid-September. *RJC*

Long-billed Dowitcher
adult summer Note strongly barred sides of breast, and entirely red underparts; long bill suggests a female. Texas, mid-April. *Arnoud B. van den Berg*

139

Long-billed Dowitcher *Limnodromus scolopaceus*
N American long-distance migrant; vagrant to Europe.
Identification L29 (11″); WS46 (18″). Medium-sized, with long (male) or very long (female), straight, pale-based and dark-tipped bill, and medium-length dull yellow or yellowish-green legs. Darkish crown, prominent supercilium and dark eye-stripe; both upperparts and underparts show considerable seasonal variation. Barred tail (not tail-coverts) has dark bars wider than white ones. Sexes of similar size, but female has longer bill; dowitchers with longest bills are female Long-billed. In flight, as Short-billed Dowitcher (p. 200). Feeds like Short-billed Dowitcher, but more often prefers fresh water.
Juvenile Brown crown, off-white supercilium; mantle, scapulars and tertials dull brown, usually lacking internal markings; mantle and scapulars have narrow, rufous, slightly scalloped fringes; tertials narrowly fringed off-white. Breast washed buff; remainder of underparts largely white.
First-winter/adult winter Very much as Short-billed Dowitcher, from which it is doubtfully distinguishable in adult plumage; grey wash on breast slightly darker and more extensive, and has more abrupt lower boundary with white belly, with less spotting. Post-juvenile moult as Short-billed, so first-winter can be aged on worn wing-coverts and specifically identified from retained juvenile scapulars or tertials.
First-summer As Short-billed Dowitcher.
Adult summer Similar to Short-billed Dowitcher. Black upperpart feathers have narrow rusty fringes; underparts entirely chestnut-red, breast (particularly sides) and much of underparts usually strongly barred black.
Call A high, thin 'keek', sometimes rapidly doubled or trebled.
Status, habitat and distribution Fairly common, breeding in Arctic beyond tree-limit, usually near fresh water; in E Siberia from 130°E, in W Alaska and NW Canada. Both Siberian and N American birds move south or southeast through Canada, some via Great Lakes, reaching Atlantic from Massachusetts south. Winters from Virginia south to Panama; rare on Atlantic coast in spring. Vagrant to Europe, mainly during mid-September to early November.
Racial variation No races recognized.
Similar species Short-billed Dowitcher.
References Nisbet 1980; Wallace 1980a; Wilds & Newlon 1983.

Eurasian Woodcock (Woodcock) *Scolopax rusticola*
Resident or migrant; vagrant to N America.
Identification L34 (13.5″); WS58 (23″). Large, short-necked, bulky, with greyish-brown, cryptically patterned plumage; long, straight, dark-tipped and pinkish-based bill and very short flesh-coloured legs. Similar plumages at all ages. Plain greyish forehead; dark eye set well back on head; rear crown and nape brown, with transverse pale bars; dark line from bill to eye. Upperparts rusty-brown and black, with some buffish feather fringes and tips; underparts buff, with dull greyish-brown barring. Sexes of similar size. In flight, uniformly dark above and below; broad, rounded wings; legs do not extend beyond tail. Feeds in or near damp woodland, both picking and probing.
Age No known characters for ageing in the field.
Call Generally silent outside breeding season.
Status, habitat and distribution Breeds in dampish woodland in Scandinavia and N USSR, south to France, N Spain, Italy and Bulgaria. Winters Britain, Ireland and Denmark south to Mediterranean; rarely in N Africa. Vagrant to Iceland, Greenland and eastern N America.
Racial variation No races recognized.
Similar species American Woodcock is smaller, more rufous beneath, and in flight its short and narrow outer primaries generate a twittering noise.

Eurasian Woodcock
Virtually impossible
to age in the field.
E England, mid-
March. *Roger Tidman*

American Woodcock *Scolopax minor*

N American resident or short-distance migrant.

Identification L28 (11″); WS42 (16.5″). Medium-sized, short-necked, bulky, with rufous-brown, cryptically patterned plumage; very long, straight pinkish-based bill and very short flesh-coloured legs. Similar plumages at all ages. Plain greyish forehead; dark eye set well back on head; rear crown and nape dark brown, with transverse pale bars; narrow dark eye-stripe. Upperparts black with rufous feather fringes and bars; broad pale grey mantle and scapular *V*s; underparts uniformly plain reddish-buff. Female typically 5% larger than male. In flight, is uniformly dark above; below, reddish-buff of underparts extends to underwing-coverts; primaries and secondaries grey-brown; outer three primaries are shortened and emarginated, producing a twittering noise; legs do not extend beyond tail. Feeds in or near damp woodlands by picking and probing.

Age No known characters for ageing in the field.

Call Generally silent outside breeding season.

Status, habitat and distribution Breeds in dampish, young woodland in eastern N America from Manitoba to Newfoundland, south to Louisiana and Florida; generally winters in south of breeding range. No European records.

Racial variation No races recognized.

Similar species Common Snipe, Great Snipe and Eurasian Woodcock.

American Woodcock
No known characters for ageing; on nest. Illinois, date not known. *Ron Austing/ Frank Lane*

Black-tailed Godwit *Limosa limosa*

European migrant; vagrant to N America.

Identification L40 (16"); WS66 (26"). Large, with long neck; very long, straight or very slightly upturned bill with dark tip and pinkish base; long dark grey legs. General coloration varies with age and season. Female marginally larger, with slightly longer bill. In flight (p. 200), darkish above, with prominent white wing-bar, white rump/uppertail-coverts and black tail; below, wing white, outlined black, with translucent wing-bar; feet and legs extend beyond tail. Feeds, often in flocks, by vertical probing, frequently wading quite deeply.

Juvenile Head and face bright buff, rather plain, with whitish supercilium, latter broader in front of eye. Mantle dark grey, scapulars black, all broadly fringed buff; tertials blackish-brown with internal buff markings and buff fringes. Underparts darkish buff, but vent paler.

First-winter/adult winter Uniformly greyish above, with short whitish supercilium; breast and flanks light grey, remainder of underparts white. First-winter retains some juvenile buff-fringed wing-coverts at least until mid-winter; adult wing-coverts are grey with faint whitish fringes.

First-summer/adult summer Very short white supercilium, white chin. Mantle and scapulars brick-red with black markings; head, neck and upper breast brick-red, the extent of red on breast depending on race. Lower breast and remainder of underparts white, barred dark brown. Underparts of female have more white and are less extensively barred. Base of bill orange-pink. First-summer attains variable amount of adult plumage.

Call A clear 'wikka-wikka-wikka'.

Status, habitat and distribution Breeds in grassy wetlands from Iceland (*L. l. islandica*), Britain, France, Netherlands and Denmark, west through central USSR (*L. l. limosa*). Typically, *islandica* winters coastally in Britain and Ireland south to the Mediterranean, and *limosa* in Africa south of Sahara. Vagrant to eastern N America.

Racial variation Juvenile *islandica* darker, more chestnut than *limosa*. Adult summer male *islandica* has red on underparts extending well on to belly; *limosa* is marginally larger and longer-billed, with light red extending less far down on underparts.

Similar species Hudsonian Godwit has slightly upturned bill, shorter legs, and, in flight, a less conspicuous white wing-bar and diagnostic sooty-black underwing-coverts. Bar-tailed Godwit is smaller, shorter-legged, has more upturned bill, and, in flight, lacks wing-bar and has white rump extending in V up back.

Reference Beintema & Drost 1986.

Black-tailed Godwit
juvenile Aged by
neat, pale-fringed,
darkish-centred
upperparts and warm
buff-washed neck
and upper breast.
Ireland, late August.
Richard T. Mills

Black-tailed Godwit
adult winter Aged
by uniform plain
upperparts and wing-
coverts. Gambia,
early January. *RJC*

Black-tailed Godwit
adult summer Male
in fresh summer
plumage; race
limosa. Netherlands,
early May. *R. Pop*

Black-tailed Godwit
adult summer
Female. Austria, late
June. *Gordon
Langsbury*

Hudsonian Godwit *Limosa haemastica*

A long-distance N American migrant; vagrant to Europe.

Identification L39 (15.5″); WS66 (26″). Large, with long neck; long, very slightly upturned bill with dark tip and pinkish base; medium-length blackish legs. White supercilium, strongest in front of eye; dark line from bill to eye. General coloration varies with age and season. Female slightly larger, with longer bill. In flight (p. 201), dark above, with short, narrow white wing-bar, white rump/uppertail-coverts, blackish tail; below, axillaries and wing-coverts sooty-black, with translucent wing-bar; feet extend beyond tail. Feeds, often in flocks, by deep vertical probing, frequently wading quite deeply.

Juvenile Mantle dark brown, with narrow buff fringes; scapulars dark brown, notched buff, or buff with narrow dark brown bars; tertials dark brown, notched buff. Wing-coverts grey with dark shaft. Underparts pale; breast mottled greyish-buff, vent white.

First-winter/adult winter Uniformly greyish above; breast light grey, remainder of underparts white. First-winter retains some worn juvenile wing-coverts; adult wing-coverts are grey with faint off-white fringes.

First-summer/adult summer Upperparts black with buffish fringes; underparts brick-red, with dark brown and white barring. Female paler, with more white barrings on underparts. First-summer attains a variable amount of adult plumage.

Call 'Ta-wit', but often silent.

Status, habitat and distribution Breeds in wet meadows near tree-line, in S Alaska, NW Mackenzie and locally west of Hudson Bay. Moves south via Hudson and James Bays, then probably flies direct to northern S America; winters in S Argentina. Returns north through central N America. Uncommon away from breeding and wintering areas; very rare vagrant to W Europe.

Racial variation No races recognized.

Similar species Black-tailed Godwit; Bar-tailed Godwit.

Hudsonian Godwit
juvenile Moulting into first-winter. USA, date not known.
A. Morris/VIREO

Hudsonian Godwit
adult Moulting from adult summer to adult winter. USA, November. *R. Villani/VIREO*

Bar-tailed Godwit *Limosa lapponica*

A Eurasian and Alaskan migrant species; vagrant to N America.

Identification L39 (15″); WS65 (25.5″). Large, fairly long-necked, with long (male) or very long (female), slightly upturned bill with dark tip and pinkish base; medium-length dark greenish-grey legs. Female is very marginally larger, but has noticeably longer bill and longer legs; plumage (especially of male) varies seasonally. In flight from above (p. 201), has blackish primary coverts, but is otherwise uniform, with

147

white rump and *V* up back (*L. l. lapponica*; see below for *L. l. baueri*); feet extend just beyond tail. Feeds, often in flocks, by deep vertical probing, both while wading and on drier ground.

Juvenile Crown dark; upperparts, wing-coverts and tertials brown, notched buff and broadly fringed off-white. Upper breast streaked or washed buff; remainder of underparts white.

First-winter/adult winter Rather pale buffish-grey upperparts with darker feather centres and broad paler fringes, less patterned and less contrasty than juvenile. Breast washed buff; remainder of underparts white. First-winter retains many worn, darkish juvenile tertials and wing-coverts which contrast with paler upperparts.

First-summer Attains a variable amount of adult summer plumage, but retains many worn juvenile wing-coverts.

Adult summer *Male*: Mantle and scapulars dark brown, with red and whitish notches and fringes; entire underparts fairly uniform chestnut-red. *Female*: Much as adult winter, but mantle and scapulars have warm buff fringes; neck and breast are variably warm buff to cream.

Call Frequently silent, but groups in flight give barking 'kirruc' or 'kak'.

Status, habitat and distribution Breeds generally on low-lying tundra, from N Scandinavia discontinuously through N USSR to about 100°E (*L. l. lapponica*), and from 100°E to W and N Alaska (*L. l. baueri*). Nominate *lapponica* winters fairly commonly in estuarine environments from Britain, Ireland and Denmark southward down Atlantic seaboard to S Africa; vagrant to Iceland and east N America.

Racial variation Race *baueri* lacks white rump and *V* up back, and has underwing barred brown; thus is separable in flight from *lapponica*.

Similar species Black-tailed Godwit.

Bar-tailed Godwit
juvenile Aged by dark-centred, pale-edged upperparts and wing-coverts, and notched tertials. (See also p. 19) E England, early October. *Gordon Langsbury*

Bar-tailed Godwit
first-winter
Relatively plain adult-type upperparts, and retained juvenile wing-coverts and tertials. Legs have rusty stain. Gambia, early January. *RJC*

Bar-tailed Godwit
adult winter Aged by plain upperparts, wing-coverts and tertials. Gambia, early January. *RJC*

Bar-tailed Godwit
adult summer Fresh plumage; from locality, identified as race *baueri*. Relatively short bill suggests a male. New Zealand, early March. *Brian Chudleigh*

149

Marbled Godwit *Limosa fedoa*

N American short-distance migrant.

Identification L44 (17.5″); WS71 (28″). Large, long-necked, with very long, slightly upturned bill with dark tip and pinkish base; medium-length dark grey legs. Barred cinnamon-buff in all plumages. Sexes of similar size, but female typically has slightly longer bill. In flight from above (p. 201), uniformly cinnamon-buff with blackish primary coverts and outer primaries; uniformly cinnamon-buff beneath; feet extend beyond tail. Feeds, often in flocks, by vertical probing while wading, but on drier ground also by picking.

Juvenile/winter Creamy-buff supercilium; upperparts uniform cinnamon-buff with blackish bars, barring broader on mantle and scapulars. Underparts buff, with sparse narrow bars on flanks. Juveniles best distinguished by neat unworn feathering at a time when late-summer adults generally show at least some very worn scapulars or tertials.

Adult summer Slightly darker, more chestnut above than adult winter; belly and flanks lightly barred dark brown.

Call A loud 'ker-reck' or 'wik-wik'.

Status, habitat and distribution Fairly common, breeding in prairie wetlands in C Canada south to S Dakota, wintering California, Texas and S Carolina south to C America (uncommon in east USA); vagrant north to Nova Scotia. No European records.

Racial variation No races recognized.

Similar species Long-billed Curlew has similar cinnamon coloration, but is larger and has strongly decurved bill.

Marbled Godwit
juvenile Best aged by neat, unworn plumage, emphasized by buff-fringed wing-coverts. Montana, July. *Urban Olsson*

Marbled Godwit
adult California,
early September.
RJC

Whimbrel *Numenius phaeopus*

A migrant species occurring on both sides of N Atlantic.

Identification L43 (17″); WS76 (30″). Large, with fairly long neck; long, strongly decurved greyish bill, pink at base; medium-length bluish-grey legs. Dark crown, prominent whitish supercilium and narrow buffish crown-stripe. Female marginally larger, with longer bill. In flight from above (p. 201), brown with blackish outer wing, white rump with *V* up back (*N. p. phaeopus*) or barred, brown back and rump (*N. p. hudsonicus);* underwing-coverts whitish in *phaeopus*, brown in *hudsonicus;* feet just reach tail. Feeds by probing and picking.

Juvenile Crown dark, with rather indistinct crown-stripe; scapulars, wing-coverts and tertials blackish, with prominent buff lateral spots.

First-winter/adult Crown-stripe more prominent than juvenile; upperparts paler, less contrasty than juvenile, broadly but diffusely fringed and notched. First-winter is difficult to distinguish, as worn juvenile wing-coverts have reduced pale spots and fading lessens contrast.

Call A fluty, rapidly repeated 'pu', typically given about seven times.

Status, habitat and distribution Common, breeding on arctic tundra near tree-line, in Iceland, Scotland, and Scandinavia to W USSR (*N. p. phaeopus*), and in Alaska and S Hudson Bay (*N. p. hudsonicus*). Nominate *phaeopus* winters coastally from Portugal and Spain to W and S Africa, a vagrant to eastern N America; *hudsonicus* winters from N Carolina south to southern S America, a rare vagrant to Europe.

Racial variation See flight notes; *hudsonicus* is darker, with more contrasting head pattern and slightly longer bill than *phaeopus*.

Similar species Western and Long-billed Curlews; Whimbrel is smaller, has shorter bill, striped head, and more barred underwing.

Whimbrel
juvenile Aged by large pale feather-edge spots contrasting with dark feather centres on upperparts, wing-coverts and tertials; long bill suggests a female. Race *phaeopus*. Ireland, early October.
Richard T. Mills

Whimbrel
first-winter Retains some pale-notched juvenile wing-coverts; short bill suggests a male. Race *phaeopus*. Gambia, early January. *RJC*

Whimbrel
adult winter Diffuse pale-brown-notched tertials are typical adult feathers; race *phaeopus*. Gambia, mid-January. *RJC*

Whimbrel
adult summer A typical late-summer migrant in very worn plumage; long bill suggests a female. Race *phaeopus.* N Wales, mid-August. *RJC*

Whimbrel
adult winter Race *hudsonicus*; note strong head pattern. Florida, mid-September. *RJC*

Slender-billed Curlew
adult winter Morocco, January. *Arnoud B. van den Berg* (See p. 155)

Western Curlew (Curlew) *Numenius arquata*

European and Asiatic migrant; vagrant to N America.

Identification L55 (21.5"); WS92 (36"). Very large, long-necked, with long (male) or very long (female), strongly decurved dark brown bill with pinkish base to lower mandible; medium-length grey legs. Sexes of similar size, but females typically have considerably longer bills. In flight from above (p. 202), has blackish primary coverts and outer primaries; white rump and *V* up back; tail barred brown; feet just reach tail. Feeds both in dampish grassland and in estuarine environments, probing deeply; sometimes wades.

Juvenile Head finely streaked dark brown; mantle and scapulars dull brown, neatly fringed warm buff, less deeply notched and lacking black barring of adult; tertials dull brown with rounded buff notches; wing-coverts rather uniform brown, fringed pale buff, giving overall chequered pattern. Neck, breast and flanks washed warm buff, neatly streaked dark brown; remainder of underparts white. Bill often shorter than that of adult.

First-winter Retains a variable number of juvenile scapulars, wing-coverts and, particularly, tertials, often showing chequered pattern of juvenile. Underparts as adult.

Adult winter Head greyish, finely streaked dark grey-brown; mantle and scapulars have blackish centres and lateral bars, with greyish-brown fringes; tertials are greyish-brown, with dark brown along shaft and dark brown oblique bars; wing-coverts dull brown, with blackish bars and extensive pale notches and fringes. Neck, breast and flanks have buffish wash with bold dark brown streaks and spots; remainder of underparts white.

Adult summer As adult winter, but head warmer buff; mantle and scapulars have blackish centres and more rufous fringes.

Call 'Cur-lee' or 'cour-loo'.

Status, habitat and distribution Common, breeding in temperate to sub-arctic dampish open areas, often moorland, from Britain and Ireland, France, Scandinavia east to Urals (*N. a. arquata*), and through Asia to about 125°E (*N. a. orientalis*). Winters both coastally and inland: *arquata* from Iceland, Britain, Ireland and Denmark south to W Africa, *orientalis* in Mediterranean (where overlaps with *arquata*) and Africa (not NW). Rare vagrant to east N America.

Racial variation In comparison with *arquata, orientalis* is larger, with longer bill, and has some brown barring on rump, streaked rather than spotted underparts, and unbarred white underwing and axillaries (p. 202), but differences are clinal.

Similar species Whimbrel. Long-billed Curlew is typically longer-billed, has general cinnamon coloration, and in flight lacks white above and has cinnamon underwing. Slender-billed Curlew *N. tenuirostris* is smaller (L39 (15″), WS79 (31″): slightly smaller than Whimbrel), has shorter, more tapered bill, extensive rounded spots on otherwise white underparts, particularly on flanks (but juvenile is streaked, not spotted, beneath), and has entirely white underwing-coverts. See photographs, p. 153 and p. 201.

References Marchant 1984; Porter 1984.

Western Curlew
adult summer
Moulting to adult winter; relatively short bill indicates a male. N Wales, early August. *RJC*
Insert *juvenile* Neatly streaked throat and breast; relatively short bill. N Wales, mid-August. *RJC*

Western Curlew
adult summer
Moulting to adult winter; relatively long bill indicates a female. N Wales, early August. *RJC*

Long-billed Curlew *Numenius americanus*

N American short-distance migrant.

Identification L57 (22.5″); WS87 (34″). Very large, long-necked, with very long, strongly decurved bill with pink base to lower mandible; medium-length grey legs. Cinnamon body with darker upperparts. Sexes of similar size, but female typically has considerably longer bill. In flight from above (p. 202), fairly uniform, though with darker forewing and blackish primary coverts and outer primaries; below, uniformly cinnamon; feet extend just beyond tail. Feeds by both picking and probing deeply; wades.

Juvenile Mantle and scapulars, and tertials blackish-brown, extensively notched buffish-cinnamon; neck, upper breast and flanks lightly streaked. Newly fledged birds have relatively short bills. Very similar to adult; best distinguished by neat, unworn plumage.

First-winter/adult Mantle and scapulars black, extensively notched cinnamon; tertials have dark narrow bars and centre line; first-winter retains some juvenile tertials. Neck, breast and flanks have dark brown streaks.

Call 'Cur-lee', with upward inflexion.

Status, habitat and distribution Breeds in grassland from British Columbia and Saskatchewan south to Texas: *N. a. parvus* Oregon to S Dakota northwards, *N. a. americana* to south. Winters from California east to Louisiana and south to Mexico, and S Carolina to Florida, where it is uncommon. No European records.

Racial variation Mainly clinal, *parvus* being the smaller.

Similar species Marbled Godwit.

Long-billed Curlew
juvenile Aged by
notched tertials and
shortish bill, and
generally unworn
plumage. N Dakota,
early September.
Claudia Wilds

Long-billed Curlew
adult Extremely
long bill suggests a
female. California,
October/November.
Eric & David Hosking

Upland Sandpiper *Bartramia longicauda*
N American long-distance migrant; vagrant to Europe.
Identification L30 (12″); WS53 (21″). Medium-sized, with small head, long neck, short straight dark bill with yellow base to lower mandible; medium-length yellow legs. Tail extends well beyond folded wings. Dark crown contrasts with plain face and prominent dark eye; brownish above, whitish underparts. Sexes of similar size. In flight, dark above (p. 202) with blackish primary coverts, primaries and secondaries, and black rump with narrow white sides; feet do not extend beyond long tail. Feeds in grassland by picking in plover-like manner, with alternating short runs and sudden stops.
Juvenile Mantle and scapulars dull brown with darker markings and narrow buff fringes; tertials dull brown, notched pale buff, with dark brown spots between notches; wing-coverts are fringed buff, with all-dark centres or U-shaped dark markings with buff centres. Underparts pale buff, throat and upper breast streaked brown; flanks have brown chevrons and bars.
First-winter Acquires adult-type mantle and scapulars, but retains most of its juvenile wing-coverts and tertials.
Adult Mantle and scapulars blackish with buffish fringes, the longer scapulars and tertials having evenly spaced black chevron bars across feathers; median coverts have black subterminal anchor marks. Underparts as juvenile. Has a very restricted spring moult and consequently retains the same plumage throughout year.
Call A mellow, liquid 'ch-wut' and a whistled 'quip-ip-ip-ip'.
Status, habitat and distribution Breeds inland in temperate and sub-arctic open grassland in Alaska and Yukon, and from British Columbia south to Oregon in the west, eastwards through the Plains and Great Lakes to W Virginia and Maryland. Uncommon in east N America; most migrate overland through the interior. Rare vagrant to Europe, most usually September–October.
Racial variation No races recognized.
Similar species None.

Upland Sandpiper
juvenile Aged by darkish-centred, pale-fringed upperparts and wing-coverts.
SW England, mid-October. *Gordon Langsbury*

Upland Sandpiper
adult Aged by barred scapulars and wing-coverts. New Jersey, early June. *F.K. Schleicher/ VIREO*

Spotted Redshank *Tringa erythropus*

A European and Asiatic migrant species; vagrant to N America.
Identification L30 (12″); WS52 (20.5″). Medium-sized, with long neck, long, straight fine bill with red base to lower mandible, and long red legs. Narrow white eye-ring. Plumage varies seasonally; adult summer has unique black body with white-spotted upperparts. Sexes of similar size. In flight, is uniformly darkish grey above, with a white *V* up back and a barred tail; feet extend beyond tail. Generally feeds in fresh water, wading fairly deeply (sometimes swimming), probing and scything, often in small flocks.
Juvenile Greyish crown; prominent off-white supercilium in front of eye only; dark eye-stripe. Upperparts and wing-coverts greyish-brown,

all strongly spotted white; underparts whitish, with throat, foreneck and upper breast mottled grey-brown, remainder strongly barred grey-brown. Legs orange-red.

First-winter/adult winter Crown brownish-grey; white supercilium in front of eye only; dark eye-stripe. Mantle, scapulars and wing-coverts grey, with narrow white fringes; tertials grey, spotted and fringed white. Underparts white, with pale grey wash across upper breast. First-winter retains many worn juvenile wing-coverts. Legs red.

First-summer Only partially attains adult summer plumage.

Adult summer Head, neck and entire underbody sooty-black; breast, and underparts from flanks to undertail-coverts have white fringes of variable extent, females showing more white than males. Mantle, scapulars and most tertials, together with a variable number of wing-coverts, black with prominent white spots. Legs darkish red.

Call A distinctive, clear 'chu-wit', with rising inflexion.

Status, habitat and distribution Fairly common; breeds on wooded to open arctic tundra from N Scandinavia throughout N USSR. Winters in Europe in small numbers on fresh water or sheltered estuaries southwards from S Britain, Ireland and Netherlands; many more occur in Africa just south of Sahara; also throughout S Asia. Rare vagrant to eastern N America.

Racial variation No races recognized.

Similar species Distinguished from Common Redshank by barred underparts of juvenile, unique adult summer plumage, and, in winter, by more elegant appearance together with prominent pale fore-supercilium and longer, finer bill. In flight, lacks white secondaries of Common Redshank.

Spotted Redshank
juvenile Generally darkish, with spotted upperparts and tertials and irregularly barred underparts.
E England, August.
Roger Tidman

Spotted Redshank
adult winter
Uniformly fresh
upperparts and
tertials. E England,
mid-September. *RJC*

Spotted Redshank
adult summer
Finland, mid-June.
J.F. Reynolds

Spotted Redshank
adult Moulting from
adult summer to
adult winter; often
seen on southward
migration in this
plumage state.
E England, late July.
RJC

Common Redshank *Tringa totanus*

European and Asiatic migrant and resident species.

Identification L28 (11"); WS51 (20"). Medium-sized, with fairly long neck, medium-length, straight horn-coloured red-based bill, and medium-length red legs. Brown or greyish-brown above with paler underparts; eye-ring white. Sexes of similar size. In flight from above (p. 202), has unique pattern of broad white trailing edge to inner wing, formed by white-tipped inner primaries and white secondaries, and white rump and *V* up back; feet project beyond tail. Feeds at fresh water and on coastal mudflats by picking and probing; often wades.

Juvenile Dark crown, sparsely streaked buff; indistinct buff supercilium; upperparts and wing-coverts dark greyish-brown, with feather edges extensively spotted buff; foreneck and upper breast white with dark brown streaks. Colour of bill base varies with increasing age from brownish to dull red; legs orange-red.

First-winter/adult winter Crown brownish-grey; upperparts and wing-coverts uniformly brownish-grey, with relatively inconspicuous small dark spots at feather edges, and, especially in fresh plumage, with narrow white fringes; foreneck and upper breast washed grey, with dark brown streaks. First-winter retains some worn juvenile wing-coverts and tertials. Base of bill and legs orange-red.

First-summer/adult summer Acquires a variable proportion of plain brownish winter-type feathers mixed with strongly brown-barred buffish feathers on both upperparts and wing-coverts. White underparts are heavily streaked brown, sometimes with brown barring on the flanks. Base of bill and legs are bright orange-red. First-summer occasionally identifiable, but only if some very worn juvenile wing-coverts or tertials are retained. During moult to adult winter plumage often shows the diagnostic white secondaries at rear of folded wing.

Call Most frequent is a fluty 'teu-tu-tu', given in flight.

Status, habitat and distribution Common; nests in temperate open, wet grasslands, in Iceland (*T. t. robusta*), Britain and Ireland, Scandinavia, locally around the Mediterranean (*T. t. totanus*), and eastwards throughout USSR south of 60°N (other races). In winter generally coastal, occurring from breeding areas south to Africa, and throughout southern Asia. No N American records.

Racial variation Race *robusta* is slightly larger and typically has a larger proportion of barred 'summer-plumage' feathers on upperparts than does *totanus*, but there is a considerable variation between individuals.

Similar species Spotted Redshank.

Common Redshank
juvenile Aged by extensively edge-spotted upperparts, wing-coverts and tertials, and orange (not red) legs.
E England, mid-July.
RJC

Common Redshank
first-summer In winter-type plumage, but acquiring a few adult summer darker breast feathers; presumably (noting worn tertials) a first-summer bird.
E England, early May. *RJC*

Common Redshank
adult summer Many dark body feathers both above and below; from location, identified as race *totanus*. E England, early July. *RJC*

Marsh Sandpiper *Tringa stagnatilis*

Migratory E European and Asiatic species.

Identification L23 (9″); WS42 (16.5″). Medium-sized, with long neck, long, fine straight bill and very long greenish or yellowish legs. Brown or grey above and white below; may show a dark area near bed of folded wing. Sexes of similar size. In flight from above (p. 203), wings sooty-grey with paler secondaries, white *V* up back, white rump and tail, the latter lightly barred in the centre; feet and legs extend beyond tail. Feeds in freshwater areas by picking, often wading, occasionally running fast through water after prey.

Juvenile Crown and hindneck brown-grey with darker streaks; white supercilium; upperparts and wing-coverts brownish-grey, with narrow dark subterminal lines and narrow white fringes; underparts white. Legs greenish.

First-winter/adult winter Very similar to juvenile, but upperparts and wing-coverts are a cleaner grey with narrower dark subterminal lines and fringes. First-winter retains some juvenile wing-coverts. Legs greenish.

First-summer Non-breeders summering in wintering areas often retain much of first-winter plumage; others return to breeding area and largely attain adult summer plumage.

Adult summer Crown and neck brownish with dark streaks: whitish supercilium; upperparts, wing-coverts and tertials brown with dark bars. Underparts white, with dark spots on upper breast; flanks spotted and barred. Legs generally yellow.

Call 'Tew'; 'chip' in alarm.

Status, habitat and distribution Breeds in open wetlands between about 48° and 58°N throughout west and central USSR. Winters in freshwater areas throughout Africa south of Sahara; also in India and SE Asia. Vagrant to W Europe north to Sweden, mainly during May and July–September; no east N American records.

Racial variation No races recognized.

Similar species Distinguished from Common Greenshank by smaller size, proportionately longer legs, and finer, straight (not slightly upturned) bill.

Marsh Sandpiper
adult winter
Uniformly brownish-grey above, white beneath. Kenya, October.
J.F. Reynolds

Marsh Sandpiper
adult summer
Extensive brown markings above; streaked neck and upper breast. W Australia, mid-August. *Brian Chudleigh*

Common Greenshank *Tringa nebularia*

European and Asiatic migrant species; vagrant to N America.

Identification L32 (12.5″); WS58 (23″). Medium-sized, elegant, with fairly long neck, medium-length, slightly upturned bill with dark tip and grey base; long yellowish-green legs. Greyish above and white beneath; narrow white eye-ring. Sexes of similar size. In flight from above (p. 203), wings uniformly grey, rump white with white *V* up back, and tail white with dark barring; feet extend beyond tail. Occurs on fresh water; feeds by wading; periodically runs after prey.

Juvenile Crown dark grey, streaked white; indistinct white supercilium. Upperparts, wing-coverts and tertials are variable, sometimes dark grey with white fringes and dark spotting on feather edges, while on others they are browner-grey with neat pale fringes, lacking spotting. Grey streaking on neck; remainder of underparts white.

First-winter/adult winter Crown and hindneck streaked dark grey, otherwise head and neck white. Upperparts grey, with neat narrow white fringes and dark subterminal lines; some dark feather-edge spotting, especially on tertials and greater coverts. Underparts white. First-winter retains many worn juvenile wing-coverts and tertials.

First-summer Extent of moult to first-summer is highly variable: some retain worn first-winter plumage, others attain near adult summer-type plumage.

Adult summer Whole of head and neck heavily streaked blackish. Mantle feathers black with narrow pale brown fringes; scapulars and tertials a mixture of pale-fringed black and uniform brownish-grey feathers, latter sometimes having dark edge spots. Upper breast and flanks heavily streaked blackish; remainder of underparts white.

Call A mellow 'teu', repeated two to four times, very similar to call of Greater Yellowlegs.

Status, habitat and distribution Fairly common; breeds in open or fairly open moorland or freshwater marshes, from Scotland eastward throughout Scandinavia and USSR, between about 53° and 68°N. Migrates south on broad front; winters in small numbers in W Europe (usually in estuarine habitats) from Scotland to Mediterranean, and more numerously at freshwater sites throughout Africa south of Sahara; also S Asia to Australia. Vagrant to Iceland; very rare vagrant to east N America.

Racial variation No races recognized.

Similar species Marsh Sandpiper; distinguished from very similar Greater Yellowlegs by duller, greenish legs, slightly more abruptly upturned bill, greyer (less brown) general coloration, and a white *V* up back in flight.

Common Greenshank
juvenile A rather strongly marked individual.
E England, mid-August. *RJC*

Common Greenshank
adult winter Neatly fringed upperparts. Gambia, early January. *RJC*

Common Greenshank
first-summer Commencing moult to adult winter; a few dark summer upperpart feathers with one or two fresh winter feathers, and extremely worn juvenile wing-coverts and tertials. E England, mid-July. *RJC*

Common Greenshank
adult summer Many dark upperpart feathers, extensively streaked breast and flanks. E England, early July. *RJC*

167

Greater Yellowlegs *Tringa melanoleuca*

N American migratory species; vagrant to Europe.

Identification L31 (12″); WS60 (23.5″). Medium-sized, with longish neck, long, slightly upturned bill with dark tip and grey base, and long bright yellow legs. Greyish-brown above and white beneath; narrow white eye-ring. Sexes of similar size. In flight, is uniformly darkish above (but secondaries show marginal buff spotting), with a white rump and barred whitish tail; feet extend well beyond tail. Generally feeds while wading.

Juvenile Streaked crown and hindneck; upperparts, wing-coverts and tertials dark grey with extensive white marginal spots, though some individuals largely lack spotting. Lower neck and upper breast white, streaked dark brown; remainder of underparts white.

First-winter/adult winter Head and upperparts much as juvenile, but mantle feathers grey-brown, edged with small spots, alternately dark and white; wing-coverts and tertials dark grey, with white edge spots. Foreneck streaked brown-grey, flanks sometimes slightly barred; remainder of underparts white. First-winter is identifiable only if retained worn juvenile wing-coverts or tertials are visible.

Adult summer Similar to juvenile, but mantle and scapulars black, fringed and edge-spotted white. Foreneck and upper breast heavily streaked black, flanks irregularly barred.

Call 'Teu', typically repeated two or three times.

Status, habitat and distribution Breeds in marshy, fairly open woodland near fresh water, in S Alaska and from British Columbia east to Labrador and Newfoundland. Migrates on broad front through N America, wintering both coastally in estuarine habitats and inland at freshwater sites from New York south, but. more commonly in southern USA and throughout S America. Vagrant to W Europe, mainly during July–November.

Racial variation No races recognized.

Similar species Common Greenshank. Distinguished from Lesser Yellowlegs by larger size and proportionately longer, heavier bill and slightly shorter legs; feathering at base of bill separated from nostril (Lesser's reaches nostril); in flight, given good view, secondaries show pale marginal spotting (Lesser's are plain).

Greater Yellowlegs
juvenile Generally greyish, with extensive white edge-spotting on upperparts, wing-coverts and tertials. California, early September. *RJC*

Greater Yellowlegs
adult winter Finer edge-spotting than juvenile, alternating dark and white. Florida, late September. *RJC*

Greater Yellowlegs
adult summer Many dark feathers in upperparts, strongly streaked and barred below. Florida, mid-April. *Gordon Langsbury*

169

Lesser Yellowlegs *Tringa flavipes*

Migratory N American species; vagrant to Europe.

Identification L24 (9.5″); WS49 (19″). Medium-sized, with longish neck, medium-length, fine, straight or very slightly upturned dark bill with greyish base, and long bright yellow legs. Brownish-grey above, white beneath; narrow white eye-ring. Sexes of similar size. In flight, is uniformly darkish above (has plain secondaries), with a white rump and barred whitish tail; feet extend well beyond tail. Feeds by picking; often wades.

Juvenile Brown-grey crown, streaked white; diffuse whitish supercilium. Upperparts, wing-coverts and tertials brownish-grey, edges of feathers extensively spotted pale buff. Foreneck streaked brownish-grey; remainder of underparts white.

First-winter/adult winter Crown, hindneck and upperparts uniform grey; wing-coverts and tertials have off-white fringes and dark side spots, the latter particularly on greater coverts and tertials. Foreneck and upper breast streaked brownish-grey; remainder of underparts white. First-winter retains some worn juvenile wing-coverts and tertials.

Adult summer Head and neck heavily streaked brown-grey; mantle and most scapulars dark brown-black, with off-white fringes and side spots, though often with a few winter-type scapulars. Upper breast heavily streaked and spotted dark brown-black, flanks sparsely barred dark brown-black; remainder of underparts white.

Call A quiet 'tu', usually given only once or twice.

Status, habitat and distribution Breeds in similar habitat to Greater Yellowlegs, from central Alaska across Canada to southern Hudson Bay and James Bay. Migrates southward on broad front; less coastal on northward passage. Winters from New York (uncommonly), more frequently in southern USA and S America south to Argentina and Chile.

Racial variation No races recognized.

Similar species See Greater Yellowlegs; distinguished from Wood Sandpiper by longer and brighter yellow legs, virtual lack of supercilium, and extension of folded wings beyond tail (wing-tips do not quite reach tail on Wood Sandpiper).

Lesser Yellowlegs
juvenile Aged by strongly spotted upperparts; tertials slightly worn, with a few grey first-winter scapulars. White staining on tibia. (See also p. 20) Florida, late September. *RJC*

Lesser Yellowlegs
adult winter Aged by unworn wing-coverts. Florida, mid-January. *RJC*

Lesser Yellowlegs
adult summer Much dark feathering above, strongly streaked neck and breast. New Jersey, July. *F.K. Schleicher/ VIREO*

Solitary Sandpiper *Tringa solitaria*

A migrant N American species; vagrant to W Europe.

Identification L20 (8″); WS42 (16.5″). Small, with straight, medium-length bill with dark tip and greenish base, and medium-length dull greenish or yellowish legs. In all plumages dark greenish-brown above, spotted whitish; white below; white eye-ring. Sexes of similar size. In flight, is uniformly dark above, with a dark rump and dark-centred tail with white barring on sides; underwings dark; feet extend just beyond tail. Feeds, in fresh or brackish water, often by wading, frequently thrusting head well under water.

Juvenile Crown brown; upperparts, wing-coverts and tertials greenish-brown with small buff marginal spots. Foreneck and upper breast indistinctly streaked brown, sides of breast barred brown. Yellow or greenish-yellow legs.

First-winter/adult winter Head and neck uniformly brown-grey; upperparts and tertials much as juvenile, though duller. First-winter retains most of its juvenile wing-coverts and some juvenile tertials, but these worn feathers are distinguished with difficulty in the field.

Adult summer Dark crown finely streaked white; upperparts, wing-coverts and tertials bronze-brown with small white spots. Throat and upper breast streaked brown, flanks diffusely barred brown; remainder of underparts white. Legs greenish.

Calls 'Peet-weet' or 'peet-weet-weet'.

Status, habitat and distribution Breeds in marshy areas with scattered trees, from central Alaska and throughout S Canada to Labrador and Quebec: *T. s. solitaria* in east as far as eastern British Columbia, and *T. s. cinnamomea* in remainder of British Columbia and further north and west. Nominate *solitaria* migrates on a broad front from mid-west states eastward, some perhaps by direct flight across W Atlantic, wintering in southern USA (rarely) and south to N Argentina and Uruguay. Vagrant to Greenland, Iceland and W Europe, typically during July–October.

Racial variation The two races are very similar, and cannot be distinguished in the field.

Similar species Green Sandpiper is slightly larger and generally very similar, and is best distinguished by its white rump which is conspicuous in flight. Spotted Sandpiper is smaller and less dark above, has a less prominent eye-ring, and has white wing-bar in flight; adult summer is spotted beneath.

Solitary Sandpiper
juvenile Most easily separated from Green Sandpiper by lack of white rump in flight. SW England, late October.
A. Cook

Solitary Sandpiper
winter Rather dull, with spotting on upperparts poorly defined. Brazil, late September. *Eric & David Hosking*

Solitary Sandpiper
adult summer Fresh plumage; strongly spotted, contrasty upperparts. Louisiana, early April. *Arnoud B. van den Berg*

Green Sandpiper *Tringa ochropus*

A migrant European and Asiatic species.

Identification L22 (9″); WS44 (17″). Medium-sized; straight, medium-length bill with dark tip and greenish base, and dull yellowish-green medium-length legs. In all plumages is dark greenish-brown above, spotted whitish; white beneath; bold white eye-ring. Sexes of similar size. In flight from above (p. 203), is uniformly dark with a bright white rump and blackish tail, latter strongly barred white across full width; feet extend just beyond tail. Feeds generally at muddy freshwater margins, often wading, thrusting head well under water.

Juvenile Crown brownish-grey; upperparts, wing-coverts and tertials have many small, dull buff marginal spots. Foreneck and upper breast brownish-grey, streaked white at centre; some barring on upper flanks; remainder of underparts white.

First-winter/adult winter Very similar to juvenile, but with slightly smaller buff spots at feather edges; foreneck and upper breast rather more streaked. First-winter retains most of its worn juvenile wing-coverts.

Adult summer Crown dark greenish-brown, streaked white; upperparts dark greenish-brown with bright white marginal spots, though not all feathers are replaced; tertials are similar, but retained worn winter feathers may lack spots. Foreneck and upper breast strongly streaked dark brown.

Call Loud, distinctive 'weet, tweet, wit, wit' on being flushed.

Status, habitat and distribution Breeds in marshy areas with scattered trees from Scandinavia through USSR to about 150°E, between 50° and 68°N. Migrates overland, wintering by fresh water, often inland, from central England and Netherlands south to C Africa. No eastern N American records.

Racial variation No races recognized.

Similar species Solitary Sandpiper. Distinguished from Wood Sandpiper by slightly greater bulk, lack of supercilium, prominent white eye-ring, darker and less strongly spotted upperparts, and, in flight, almost black and white flight pattern enhanced by the dark underwing. Common Sandpiper is smaller and less dark above, has a less prominent eye-ring, and has white wing-bar and dark rump in flight.

Green Sandpiper
juvenile Pale buff feather-edge spotting to upperparts, wing-coverts and tertials; head, neck and upper breast washed olive-brown.
E England, early September. *RJC*

Green Sandpiper
adult winter Whitish-buff feather-edge spotting to upperparts, wing-coverts and tertials; upper breast more streaked than on juvenile. Retains one or two worn, white-spotted adult summer scapulars.
E England, mid-August. *RJC*

Green Sandpiper
adult summer Worn plumage; larger white spots on upperparts, worn tertials, and heavily streaked head, neck and upper breast.
E England, early July. *RJC*

Wood Sandpiper *Tringa glareola*

A strongly migratory European and Asiatic species; vagrant to N America.

Identification L20 (8"); WS39 (15.5"). Small; medium-length, straight bill with dark tip and dull greenish base; long dull yellowish or greenish legs. Prominent creamy supercilium; off-white eye-ring; brown upperparts with copious fairly large pale spots; white underparts. Sexes of similar size. In flight from above (p. 203), uniform brown (outer primary shaft white) with white rump and barred-brown tail; underwing off-white; feet project beyond tail. Feeds by picking at muddy freshwater margins.

Juvenile Crown brownish-black with creamy streaks; upperparts brown with cream marginal spots and fringes, wing-coverts and tertials strongly spotted cream. Upper breast lightly mottled brown; remainder of underparts white, but with sparse brown streaking on undertail-coverts.

First-winter/adult winter Much as juvenile, but pale spots and fringes on upperparts duller and slightly less conspicuous. Foreneck and breast streaked and washed brownish-grey. First-winter retains some worn juvenile wing-coverts and tertials, but is difficult to distinguish from adult.

Adult summer Similar to juvenile, but upperparts and replaced tertials and wing-coverts are darker brown, with prominent white spots. Throat white, foreneck and breast strongly streaked dark brown, flanks barred brown.

Call A sharp, high-pitched 'chiff-iff-iff'.

Status, habitat and distribution Breeds in marshland, usually in areas with some trees, from Scotland (rare), Denmark, Scandinavia and through N USSR to about 170°E, between 50° and 70°N. Migrates on broad front, wintering in N Africa (small numbers) and inland in Africa south of Sahara; also throughout S Asia to Australia. Scarce in Wales and Ireland, particularly in spring; vagrant to Iceland and Greenland; very rare vagrant to east N America.

Racial variation No races recognized.

Similar species Lesser Yellowlegs; Green Sandpiper.

Wood Sandpiper
juvenile Aged by relatively large pale spots on upperparts and tertials; note prominent supercilium. N Wales, mid-August. *RJC*

Wood Sandpiper
first-winter Less strongly spotted; retains worn juvenile tertials. Gambia, mid-January. *RJC*

Wood Sandpiper
adult summer Darker, strongly spotted upperparts; heavily streaked neck, upper breast and flanks.
E England, May. *Roger Tidman*

Common Sandpiper *Actitis hypoleucos*

A migratory European and Asiatic species.

Identification L20 (8"); WS34.5 (13.5"). Small; straight, medium-length brownish bill with dark tip, and short dull yellow (sometimes greyish) legs. Brown above, white beneath, with sharply demarcated brown area on upper breast. Tail extends well beyond tips of folded wings. Sexes of similar size. In flight from above (p. 203), brown with narrow white wing-bar across secondaries and inner primaries, white trailing edge to secondaries, and white outer tail; feet do not extend beyond tail. Has characteristic low flicking flight on downward-bowed wings. Feeds generally by picking at edge of fresh water, occasionally wading; constantly bobs tail.

Juvenile Crown brown; indistinct supercilium; white eye-ring. Upperparts brown, with narrow pale brown fringes and narrow dark subterminal lines; wing-coverts brown, with pale brown tips and black-brown subterminal bars; tertials brown, with small dark spots along narrow pale brown fringes. Brown upper breast finely streaked.

First-winter/adult winter Similar to juvenile, though with fairly uniform brown upperparts; wing-coverts fringed buff at tip with darker subterminal bars, less contrasty than juvenile. Brown on upper breast less extensive and more uniformly coloured than juvenile, sometimes not meeting at centre; remainder of underparts white. Moult to first-winter often complete, thus difficult to age in winter.

Adult summer Upperparts, tertials and wing-coverts bronze-brown, with dark brown shaft-streaks and irregular narrow barring; brown upper breast is streaked dark brown.

Call Typically a clear, high-pitched, three-note 'swee-wee-wee'.

Status, habitat and distribution A widespread species, breeding near clear, fresh water, especially by upland streams, throughout most of Europe and N Asia to about 70°N. Migrates on a broad front, wintering mostly by fresh water locally from S England (uncommon) southwards, though most move to Africa south of the Sahara; also winters in S Asia and Australia. No east N American records.

Racial variation No races recognized.

Similar species Spotted Sandpiper is very similar, but has very short extension of tail beyond tips of folded wings (long in Common), yellow legs, and in flight has less extensive wing-bar and less white at sides of tail. Juvenile Spotted Sandpiper is greyer, has more boldly barred wing-coverts, and the spotting on the tertials and greater coverts is confined to the tips (not extending along the feather edges as on Common); adult summer Spotted Sandpiper has boldly spotted breast. Typical call of Spotted Sandpiper is softer and usually disyllabic.

References Madge 1980; Wallace 1980b.

Common Sandpiper
juvenile Aged by barred wing-coverts and edge-spotted tertials; note longish tail extension beyond wing-tips. E England, mid-August. *RJC*

Common Sandpiper
winter Duller, with unstreaked breast. Gambia, early January. *RJC*

Common Sandpiper
adult summer In worn plumage; brighter, bronze-brown, above, and some streaking on breast. N Wales, early August. *RJC*

Spotted Sandpiper *Actitis macularia*

A migrant N American species; vagrant to Europe.

Identification L19 (7.5″); WS32.5 (13″). Small, with medium-length brown bill and short yellowish or flesh-coloured legs. Brown above, white beneath (spotted in adult summer), with sharply demarcated brown area on upper breast. Tail extends only a short distance beyond tips of folded wings. Sexes of similar size. In flight from above (p. 203), brown, with restricted white wing-bar across inner primaries and outer secondaries, white trailing edge to secondaries and white outer tail; feet do not extend beyond tail. Has characteristic low flicking flight on downward-bowed wings. Feeds generally by picking at edge of fresh water, occasionally wading; constantly bobs tail.

Juvenile Crown brown; indistinct supercilium; white eye-ring. Upperparts greyish-brown, with buff fringes and narrow dark subterminal lines; wing-coverts brown, with tips strongly barred pale buff and dark brown; greater coverts and tertials uniform brown, barred only at tip. Brown upper breast almost unstreaked, paler at centre. Bill pinkish with dark tip; legs yellowish-flesh to bright yellow.

First-winter/adult winter As juvenile, but with fairly uniform brown upperparts; wing-coverts fringed buff at tip, with darker subterminal bars; much less contrasty than juvenile. First-winter may retain some worn wing-coverts. Bill brown with pinkish lower mandible; legs variably pale grey, yellowish or flesh.

Adult summer Upperparts, tertials and wing-coverts bronze-brown, with dark brown irregular bars and shaft-streaks; upper breast washed brown; irregular round dark brown spots on underparts from throat to vent. Bill pinkish-orange with dark tip; legs pink.

Call Typically a disyllabic 'peet-weet', less clear than call of Common Sandpiper.

Status, habitat and distribution Breeds in open areas near fresh water, in Alaska, throughout Canada except far north, and in USA south to California and S Carolina. Winters from southern USA south to Chile and Argentina. Vagrant to W Europe.

Racial variation No races recognized.

Similar species Common Sandpiper.

References Madge 1980; Wallace 1980b.

Spotted Sandpiper
juvenile Strongly
barred wing-coverts,
lack of edge-spotting
on tertials, and
yellow legs aid
separation from
juvenile Common
Sandpiper.
SW England, late
August. *J.B. & S.
Bottomley*

Spotted Sandpiper
winter Relatively
uniform plumage;
note short extension
of tail beyond wing-
tips. Florida, mid-
January. *RJC*

Spotted Sandpiper
adult summer Note
bill pattern compared
with that of Common
Sandpiper. Florida,
early May. *Gordon
Langsbury*

Willet *Catoptrophorus semipalmatus*

A migrant N American species; vagrant to Europe.

Identification L37 (14.5″); WS63 (25″). Large, long-necked, with heavy, medium-length grey-based and black-tipped straight bill and long grey legs. Narrow white eye-ring. Sexes of similar size. In flight from above (p. 204), has striking wing pattern of broad white wing-bar, black primary coverts, grey inner wing-coverts, and black trailing edge which is broad on outer primaries but extends only to outer secondaries; inner secondaries white; white rump, greyish tail; feet extend beyond tail. Feeds by picking and probing, sometimes wading.

Juvenile Upperparts and wing-coverts grey-brown, fringed buff, with dark subterminal lines; tertials notched buff. Upper breast washed brownish; remainder of underparts white.

First-winter/adult winter Uniform pale grey upperparts and wing-coverts have narrow paler fringes when fresh. Breast washed pale grey; remainder of underparts white. First-winter retains many worn juvenile wing-coverts.

Adult summer Upperparts light brown, strongly barred dark brown. Neck, breast and flanks strongly streaked and barred brown.

Call 'Kip', and 'pill-will-willet'.

Status, habitat and distribution Breeds in coastal saltmarsh in Nova Scotia, from New Jersey south to Florida, the Gulf of Mexico and northern S America (*C. s. semipalmatus*), and in prairie marshes in W Canada and W USA (*C. s. inornatus*). Winters from N Carolina to Brazil, and from Oregon to Peru. Very rare vagrant to Europe.

Racial variation Only distinguishable in adult summer plumage. Nominate *semipalmatus* is described above; *inornatus* is slightly larger and paler, with less streaking and barring on breast and flanks.

Similar species None.

Willet
juvenile Aged by strongly patterned upperparts, wing-coverts and tertials; has already acquired a few first-winter upperparts. Florida, late September. *RJC*

Willet
first-winter Heavily worn and faded wing-coverts. Florida, mid-January. *RJC*

Willet
adult winter Florida, mid-January. *RJC*

Willet
adult summer Showing strongly barred underparts of race *semipalmatus*. Florida, late March. *Gordon Langsbury*

Ruddy Turnstone (Turnstone) *Arenaria interpres*

A migrant species of almost worldwide occurrence.

Identification L24 (9″); WS48 (19″). Medium-sized, with short neck, short black-tipped grey bill and short orange legs. Seasonally variable plumage, but always has distinctive black or brown breast containing pale or white areas; remainder of underparts white. In flight from above (p. 204), dark, with striking pattern of white up back, white area parallel to body at base of wing, white wing-bar and uppertail-coverts, and white outline to black tail; feet do not reach tail-tip. Feeds in a variety of coastal habitats, particularly on rocky shores, using bill to turn stones and weed.

Juvenile Crown brown, streaked darker; upperparts, tertials and wing-coverts blackish-brown, with neat off-white or buff fringes. Face and throat white with brown ear-coverts. Breast patches generally brownish.

First-winter/adult winter Head and face greyish; chin and throat white; upperparts, wing-coverts and tertials dark greyish-brown, shading paler at margins. Pale brownish breast patches. First-winter retains most of its worn juvenile wing-coverts and some juvenile tertials.

First-summer Non-breeding birds, which have a mixture of adult summer and worn first-winter plumage, are not uncommon away from the breeding areas.

Adult summer Crown white, streaked black; remainder of head and neck white, with striking black markings contiguous with black breast; white breast patches. Mantle and scapulars largely black, but have a broad line of bright rusty-chestnut running across scapulars. The extent of black streaking on crown is variable, but in breeding pairs the male has a whiter crown and is generally brighter than the female.

Call A rapid, low-pitched, musical rattle, 'tuk-a-tuk-tuk'.

Status, habitat and distribution Common, breeding coastally near rocky or pebbly shores, with a circumpolar distribution. *A. i. interpres* breeds in NE Canadian islands, Greenland, and from Denmark and Norway through USSR to Alaska; *A. i. morinella* in N Canada. Does not breed in Iceland. Winters coastally world-wide, in and south of the temperate zone.

Racial variation Nominate *interpres* is described above; *morinella* is slightly smaller, and generally brighter in all plumages. Juvenile *morinella* has pale chestnut fringes to upperparts and wing-coverts, shading rufous towards margins; adult summer has whiter crown and more extensive brighter chestnut area on upperparts.

Similar species The closely related Black Turnstone *A. melanocephala* of western N America has not occurred in the N Atlantic area.

Ruddy Turnstone
juvenile Neat pale
fringes to upperparts,
wing-coverts and
tertials; race
interpres.
SW England, early
September. *RJC*

Ruddy Turnstone
juvenile Race
morinella; note more
rufous wing-coverts
than on juvenile of
race *interpres.*
Georgia, late
September. *David
Tomlinson*

Ruddy Turnstone
first-winter Plain
upperparts, but
retains pale-fringed
juvenile wing-coverts;
race *interpres.*
N Wales, early
November. *RJC*

185

Ruddy Turnstone
first-winter Aged by
remaining worn
juvenile wing-coverts;
note more rufous
tones of race
morinella. Florida,
mid-January. *RJC*

Ruddy Turnstone
adult summer In
fresh plumage; race
morinella. Florida,
mid-April. *Gordon
Langsbury*

Ruddy Turnstone
adult summer In
worn plumage; race
interpres. N Wales,
mid-August. *RJC*

Wilson's Phalarope *Phalaropus tricolor*

A migratory N American species; vagrant to Europe.

Identification L23 (9"); WS40 (16"). Medium-sized, with long neck, needle-fine, straight black bill with greenish base, and medium-length legs. Plumages vary seasonally; female slightly larger than male. In flight from above (p. 204), fairly uniform, with white rump and uppertail-coverts; feet extend beyond tail. Feeds by swimming in typical phalarope manner (p. 22), but also by picking on mud, or by wading.

Juvenile Crown dark brown; white supercilium. Upperparts, wing-coverts and tertials black or blackish, with neat buff or whitish fringes. Entire underparts white. Legs bright yellow.

First-winter/adult winter Crown grey; white supercilium, sometimes in front of eye only. Upperparts, wing-coverts and tertials grey, with narrow white fringes; entire underparts white; legs bright yellow, gradually darkening through winter. First-winter usually retains worn juvenile wing-coverts.

Adult summer *Female*: Whitish forehead; light grey crown, hindneck, nape and mantle; black running from lores, ear-coverts and side of neck to edge of mantle, forming indistinct mantle *V*; chestnut area across lower scapulars. Chin and throat white, foreneck pinkish-buff; remainder of underparts white. Legs black. *Male*: Duller than female; grey of head, neck and underparts replaced by brown; small white area in front of eye; otherwise as female.

Call Generally silent except when breeding.

Status, habitat and distribution Uncommon in N Atlantic area; breeds in interior SW Canada and NW USA and around Great Lakes, migrating south overland to winter in southern S America. Vagrant to Europe, most frequently during late August to mid-October.

Racial variation No races recognized.

Similar species Distinguished from the other two phalarope species by larger size, proportionately longer bill, yellow or black legs, absence of eye-patch in non-breeding plumages, and distinctive flight pattern. From Lesser Yellowlegs by lack of spotting on upperparts in any plumage.

Wilson's Phalarope
juvenile Aged by
brown upperparts.
California, July.
P. Scova Righini

Wilson's Phalarope
first-winter Grey
upperparts with
narrow white fringes;
browner retained
juvenile wing-coverts
and tertials.
California, July.
P. Scova Righini

Wilson's Phalarope
adult summer
Female. Alberta,
May. *D.A. Smith*

Wilson's Phalarope
adult summer Male.
Alberta, May. *D.A.
Smith*

Red-necked Phalarope *Phalaropus lobatus*

A migratory species occurring on both sides of the N Atlantic.
Identification L18 (7″); WS34 (13.5″). Small, with longish neck, short, straight, needle-fine black bill, and short yellowish or grey legs. Plumages vary seasonally. Female slightly larger than male. In flight from above (p. 204), has white wing-bar formed by tips to greater coverts, extending narrowly on to tips of primary coverts; white sides to rump and uppertail-coverts; feet do not extend beyond dark tail; beneath, white underwing-coverts contrast with grey flight feathers. Feeds by picking from the water surface while swimming (p. 22).
Juvenile Forehead, crown, nape and hindneck dark grey; dark patch through eye to ear-coverts. Upperparts, wing-coverts and tertials dark grey, with neat buff fringes. Chin, throat and underparts white, foreneck sometimes pinkish. Legs initially yellow, becoming grey.
First-winter/adult winter Whitish head with greyish crown and black patch through eye; upperparts, wing-coverts and tertials grey, with narrow white fringes; underparts white. Legs dark grey. First-winter retains a variable number of worn juvenile wing-coverts. (Full first-winter plumage is not often seen in N Atlantic, as most birds of the year move south and complete the post-juvenile moult in the wintering area.)
Adult summer *Female*: Dark grey head and neck, with tiny white spot over eye; white chin and throat; red of foreneck and side of neck extends around rear of ear-coverts. Upperparts, wing-coverts and tertials black or grey, with warm buff fringes, and broad warm buff mantle *V*. Breast and flanks grey; remainder of underparts white. Legs dark grey. *Male*: Similar to female, but generally duller.

Call A sharp 'whit', and 'kerrek, kerrek'.

Status, habitat and distribution Uncommon; breeds in wet marshy areas of Arctic, having circumpolar distribution northwards from Norway, Scotland and Iceland in Europe, in S Greenland, and from Labrador northwards in Canada; also in Alaska and throughout N USSR. Scandinavian individuals migrate southeastwards overland, using freshwater staging posts, to winter in Arabian Sea, so is uncommon in W Europe; occurs in numbers offshore south to New York during migration, but scarcer on the coast; the majority of N American birds probably winter in the Pacific off Peru.

Racial variation No races recognized.

Similar species Wilson's Phalarope. Distinguished from Grey/Red Phalarope by slightly smaller size, longer, finer bill, and more erratic flight with more strongly marked underwing pattern.

Red-necked Phalarope
juvenile Still with black forehead, but already acquiring a few grey first-winter scapulars. Iceland, late August. *R. Pop*

Red-necked Phalarope
juvenile Head becoming white, and has more first-winter upperpart feathers; a typical plumage shown by migrants. (See also p. 22) California, mid-September. *RJC*

Red-necked Phalarope
adult summer Female. Norway, mid-June. *Gordon Langsbury*

Red-necked Phalarope
adult summer Male. Iceland, mid-August. *R. Pop*

Grey/Red Phalarope *Phalaropus fulicarius*

Widespread N Atlantic migrant; 'Grey' in Europe, 'Red' in N America.
Identification L21 (8″); WS41 (16″). Small, with longish neck, short, horizontally flattened, straight bill, and short bluish or greyish legs. Plumages vary seasonally. Female slightly larger than male. In flight from above (p. 204), has white wing-bar formed by tips to greater coverts, extending narrowly to tips of primary coverts; underwing more or less uniformly pale; feet do not extend beyond tail. Feeds by picking from the water surface while swimming (p. 22).
Juvenile Off-white forehead, brown crown; short white supercilium. Darkish around eye, but lacks dark eye-patch, which is quickly attained at start of moult to first-winter. Upperparts and tertials dark brown, neatly fringed buff; wing-coverts dark brown with whitish fringes. Throat, foreneck, breast and flanks salmon-pink; remainder of underparts white. Brownish or greyish-black bill; greyish legs.
First-winter/adult winter Forehead and fore-crown whitish; blackish patch around eye and on ear-coverts; hind-crown and hindneck grey, merging into grey upperparts which have narrow white fringes when fresh. First-winter retains many juvenile wing-coverts and tertials. Bare parts as juvenile, but bill usually has yellowish base.
Adult summer *Female*: Forehead, crown and area at base of bill black; white patch around eye and on ear-coverts. Nape and hindneck black; upperparts black with rusty and buff fringes, giving streaked appearance. Whole of underparts chestnut-red. Bill yellow with black tip; legs bluish-grey. *Male*: Duller and less contrasty than female, with more black on bill tip.
Call A whistled 'wit'.
Status, habitat and distribution Has circumpolar arctic coastal breeding distribution. Migrates south over sea, occurring inland only when storm driven, thus uncommon coastally and inland on both sides of N Atlantic. Winters in flocks offshore, in Pacific off Chile and in Atlantic off W Africa.
Racial variation No races recognized.
Similar species Red-necked Phalarope.

Grey/Red Phalarope
juvenile Has acquired a few grey first-winter upperpart feathers.
SW England, early September. *J.B. & S. Bottomley*

Grey/Red Phalarope
adult winter Uniformly grey, without retained darkish juvenile feathers.
SW England, October. *Roger Tidman*

Grey/Red Phalarope
adult summer Female. Alaska, June. *R. van Meurs*

SHOREBIRDS IN FLIGHT

The flight and wing-pattern photographs that follow show something of the variety of shorebird flight patterns, which are described in the Species Accounts. Most of the photographs illustrate the upperwing, which is generally of most value for identification, but for some species useful field marks are provided by the underwing patterns, and some of these, too, are illustrated.

Conveniently, the flight pattern of each individual species does not usually change significantly with age or plumage. Of the few species that are exceptions to this generalization, the most notable in the N Atlantic area is the Black-winged/Black-necked Stilt: the adult has an all-black wing, but first-year birds have a narrow, conspicuous white trailing edge running nearly the full length of the wing. Other species show slight changes with the seasons: the white rump of the Stilt Sandpiper, for example, has brown markings in adult summer plumage. Sometimes the flight pattern varies with different races of the same species, as with the Whimbrel, the European race of which has a white rump and back; the American race is all-brown above. Underwing patterns, too, can be critical to racial identification: for instance, the Asiatic race of the Western Curlew has unbarred white underwing-coverts and axillaries, while those of the European race are quite strongly barred.

The page numbers given in the captions refer to the detailed description of each respective species.

Northern Pied Oystercatchers *adults*, mid-April, RJC (p. 42)

Black-winged Stilts, left *first-winter*, right *adult*, mid-January. *RJC* (p. 45)

Pied Avocets, mid-March. *RJC* (p. 48)

Collared Pratincole *adult*, late July. *Arnoud B. van den Berg* (p. 54)

195

Ringed Plovers, early August.
RJC (p. 60)

Semipalmated Plover *adult,*
mid-September. *RJC* (p. 62)

Killdeer *adult summer*, May/
June. *D.A. Smith* (p. 66)

Piping Plover *juvenile,*
mid-September. *RJC* (p. 68)

Pacific Golden Plovers *moulting
into adult summer,* April. *S.C.
Madge* (p. 78)

European Golden Plovers
moulting into adult summer, early
April. *RJC* (p. 80)

Grey/Black-bellied Plover *winter*, early January. *RJC* (p. 82)

Northern Lapwing *adult summer*, male (underwing), late May. *RJC* (p. 85)

Northern Lapwing *adult summer*, female (upperwing), late May; note that male has white on four outermost primaries (three on female). *RJC* (p. 85)

Red Knots *winter*, early February. *Brian Chudleigh* (p.87)

Sanderling *winter*, mid-January.
RJC (p. 90)

Temminck's Stint *adult summer*,
June. *D.A. Smith* (p. 102)

Least Sandpiper *juvenile*, mid-
September. *RJC* (p. 106)

Baird's Sandpiper *juvenile*.
September. *Richard T. Mills* (p.110)

Pectoral Sandpiper *juvenile*, late
September. *RJC* (p. 112)

Curlew Sandpiper *winter*, early
January. *RJC* (p. 114)

Purple Sandpipers *adults*, mid-April. *RJC* (p. 116)

Dunlin *juvenile* (one of European races), mid-August. *RJC* (p. 118)

Ruff *adult*, April. *Paul Doherty* (p. 128)

Common Snipes *winter*, mid-January. *Richard T. Mills* (p. 132)

Jack Snipe, early March. *RJC* (p. 134)

Great Snipe September. *Hadoram Shirihai* (p. 135)

Dowitchers (arrowed), late March; left probably Short-billed, right probably Long-billed. *Gordon Langsbury* (pp. 136 & 140)

Black-tailed Godwits, mid-March. *RJC* (p. 143)

Hudsonian Godwits *juveniles*, August. *Urban Olsson* (p. 146)

Bar-tailed Godwit (race *lapponica*) *winter*, early January. *RJC* (p. 147)

Marbled Godwits, mid-September. *RJC* (p. 150)

Whimbrel (race *phaeopus*) *winter*, mid-January. *RJC* (p. 151)

Whimbrel (race *phaeopus*) *winter*, mid-January. *RJC* (p. 151)

Slender-billed Curlew *winter*, late January. *Arnoud B. van den Berg* (p. 155)

Western Curlew (race *arquata*), mid-August. *RJC* (p. 154)

Western Curlew (race *orientalis*), early January. *RJC* (p. 154)

Western Curlew (race *orientalis*), early January; note white axillaries. *RJC* (p. 154)

Long-billed Curlew, December. *F.K. Schleicher/VIREO* (p. 156)

Upland Sandpiper *adult*, June. *F.K. Schleicher/VIREO* (p. 158)

Common Redshank *adult summer*, mid-June. *RJC* (p. 162)

Marsh Sandpiper *winter*, mid-January. *RJC* (p. 164)

Common Greenshank *winter*, mid-January. *RJC* (p. 165)

Green Sandpiper *adult summer*, April. *Paul Doherty* (p. 174)

Wood Sandpiper *adult summer*, April. *Paul Doherty* (p. 176)

Spotted Sandpiper *juvenile*, mid-September. *RJC* (p. 180)

Common Sandpiper *winter*, mid-January. *RJC* (p. 178)

Willet *juvenile*, late September. *RJC* (p. 182)

Ruddy Turnstones *winter*, mid-April. *RJC* (p. 184)

Wilson's Phalarope *first-winter*, late August. *Richard T. Mills* (p. 187)

Wilson's Phalarope *first-winter*, mid-September. *RJC* (p. 187)

Red-necked Phalarope *juvenile*, September. *Paul Doherty* (p.189)

Grey/Red Phalarope *winter*. *Richard T. Mills* (p. 192)

REFERENCES

American Ornithologists' Union (1983) *Check List of North American Birds*, 6th Edition.

Beintema, A.J. & Drost, N. (1986) Migration of the Black-tailed Godwit. *Le Gerfaut* **76** pp. 37–62.

British Birds (1981) Bird topography. *British Birds* **74** pp. 239–42.

British Birds (1985) Plumage, age and moult terminology. *British Birds* **78** pp. 419–27.

British Ornithologists' Union Records Committee (1988) Suggested changes to the English names of some Western Palearctic birds. *British Birds* **81** pp. 355–77; *Ibis* 180 (Supplement).

Britton, D. (1980) Identification of Sharp-tailed Sandpipers. *British Birds* **73** pp. 333–45.

Chandler, R.J. (1987a) Yellow orbital ring of Semipalmated and Ringed Plovers. *British Birds* **80** pp. 241–2.

Chandler, R.J. (1987b) Mystery photographs: Semipalmated Plover. *British Birds* **80** pp. 238–41.

Chandler, R.J. (1987c) Plumages of breeding female Ruffs. *British Birds* **80** pp. 246–8.

Clark, N.A. (1987) Ageing criteria for Dunlins in the field. *British Birds* **80** pp. 242–6.

Connors, P.G. (1983) Taxonomy, distribution, and evolution of golden plovers (*Pluvialis dominica* and *Pluvialis fulva*). *Auk* **100** pp. 607–20.

Cramp, S. & Simmons, K.E.L. (eds.) (1983) *The Birds of the Western Palearctic*, Vol. III. Oxford.

Dare, P.J. & Mercer, A.J. (1974) The white collar of the Oystercatcher. *Bird Study* **21** pp. 180–4.

Dukes, P.A. (1980) Semipalmated Plover: new to Britain and Ireland. *British Birds* **73** pp. 458–64.

Ferns, P.N. & Green, G.H. (1979) Observations on the breeding plumage and prenuptial moult of Dunlins *Calidris alpina*, captured in Britain. *Le Gerfaut* **69** pp. 286–303.

Ginn, H.B. & Melville, D.S. (1983) *Moult in Birds*. BTO Guide 19, Tring.

Green, R.E. & Bowden, C.G.R. (1986) Field characters for ageing and sexing Stone-curlews. *British Birds* **79** pp. 419–22.

Greenwood, J.G. (1984) Migration of Dunlin *Calidris alpina*: a worldwide overview. *Ringing & Migration* **5** pp. 35–9.

Haig, G.M. (1983) Wintering Baird's Sandpiper at Staines Reservoir. *London Bird Report* **47** pp. 87–90.

Hale, W.G. (1980) *Waders*. London.

Hayman, P., Marchant, J.H. & Prater, A.J. (1986) *Shorebirds: an identification guide to the waders of the world*. London & Sydney.

Hill, M. & Langsbury, G. (1987) *A Field Guide to Photographing Birds*. London.

Holden, P. (1985) Measurement of wing-span. *British Birds* **78** pp. 403–4.

Humphrey, P.S. & Parkes, K.C. (1959) An approach to the study of moults and plumages. *Auk* **76** pp. 1–31.

Jonsson, L. & Grant, P.J. (1984) Identification of stints and peeps. *British Birds* **77** pp. 293–315.

Kieser, J.A. & Smith, F.T.H. (1982) Field identification of the Pectoral Sandpiper *Calidris melanotos*. *Australian Bird Watcher* **9** pp. 137–46.

Madge, S.C. (1980) Field Identification of Spotted Sandpipers. In Sharrock. J.T.R. (1980) pp. 106–9.

Marchant, J.H. (1984) Identification of Slender-billed Curlew. *British Birds* **77** pp. 135–40.

Marchant, J.H. (1985) Mystery photographs: Baird's Sandpiper. *British Birds* **78** pp. 589–90.

Nethersole-Thompson, D. & M. (1986) *Waders: their breeding, haunts and watchers.* Calton.

Nisbet, I.C.T. (1980) Dowitchers in Great Britain and Ireland. In Sharrock, J.T.R. (1980) pp. 16–31.

Paulson, D.R. (1986) Identification of juvenile tattlers, and a Grey-tailed Tattler record from Washington. *Western Birds* **17** pp 33–6.

Porter, R. (1984) Mystery photographs: Slender-billed Curlew. *British Birds* **77** pp. 581–6.

Prater, A.J. (1982) Identification of Ruff. *Dutch Birding* **4** pp. 8–14.

Prater, A.J., Marchant, J.H. & Vuorinen, J. (1977) *Guide to the Identification and Ageing of Holarctic Waders.* BTO Guide 17, Tring.

Pym, A. (1982) Identification of Lesser Golden Plover and status in Britain and Ireland. *British Birds* **75** pp. 112–24.

Reynolds, J.D. (1984) Male Ruff displays to three females near Churchill, Manitoba. *Blue Jay* **42** pp. 219–21.

Sharrock, J.T.R. (ed.) (1980) *Frontiers of Bird Identification.* London.

Turner Ettlinger, D.M. (ed.) (1974) *Natural History Photography.* London.

van den Berg, A.B. (1985) Juvenile plumage of Black-winged Pratincole. *Dutch Birding* **7** pp. 143–4.

Veit, R.R. & Jonsson, L. (1984) Field identification of smaller sandpipers within the genus *Calidris. American Birds* **38** pp. 853–76.

Vinicombe, K. (1988) Unspecific Golden Plover in Avon. *Birding World* **1** pp. 54–6.

Voous, K.H. (1973) List of recent Holarctic bird species. *Ibis* **115** pp. 612–38.

Wallace, D.I.M. (1980a) Dowitcher identification: a brief review. In Sharrock, J.T.R. (1980) pp. 78–88.

Wallace, D.I.M. (1980b) Identification of Spotted Sandpipers out of breeding plumage. In Sharrock, J.T.R. (1980) pp. 101–6.

Wallace, D.I.M. (1980c) Field identification of small species in the genus *Calidris*. In Sharrock, J.T.R. (1980) pp. 146–62.

Wallace, D.I.M. (1980d & e) Distinguishing Great Snipe from Snipe, *and* Further definition of Great Snipe characters. In Sharrock, J.T.R. (1980) pp. 225–30 and pp. 261–6.

Warham, J. (1983) *The Technique of Bird Photography*, 4th Edition. London.

Wilds, C. & Newlon, M. (1983) The identification of dowitchers. *Birding* **15** pp. 151–66.

INDEX

Page numbers in **bold** refer to the main species description; page numbers in *italic* refer to photographs.